Public Sector
Mediation

Public Sector
Mediation

Arnold M. Zack

The Bureau of National Affairs, Inc.
Washington, D.C.

Copyright © 1985
The Bureau of National Affairs, Inc.
Washington, D.C.

Library of Congress Cataloging in Publication Data

Zack, Arnold.
  Public sector mediation.

  Includes index.
  1. Collective bargaining—Government employees—
United States.   2. Mediation.   I. Title.
HD8005.6.U5Z32   1985   331.89'142   85-7702
ISBN 0-87179-477-2

International Standard Book Number: 0-87179-477-2
Printed in the United States of America

Preface

People know about mediators, and that mediation is an essential step in the labor-management process. They recognize that it means bringing in an outsider to help the disputing parties move closer together and settle their differences. But beyond that, most people have little awareness of who the mediators are, how they are designated, or what they do once they are involved in a dispute.

The public's lack of knowledge may be due in part to the fact that there is no prescribed formula for mediation. Every dispute involves different issues; the parties are different; and the mediators approach their responsibilities with different experiences and techniques. Each mediation has its own pattern. This is part of the excitement of mediation, and causes much of the confusion about what should go on in the process.

In doing their work, mediators lead rather isolated professional lives. Even if they are surrounded by people from both teams during their mediation sessions and with the press thereafter, they do their mediating alone. They alone must decide what action to take and when to act. They have no one to turn to or to advise them during their mediation efforts.

In the mid 1960s, when mediation became more prevalent in the public sector, there were no "how to" books available for those of us first venturing into this new arena. No one was more conscious than I of this isolation when I first began to mediate. I had entered the labor management field as an apprentice to Saul Wallen, then president of the National Academy of Arbitrators, after graduating from law school in 1956. My classroom education in labor relations and negotiations was augmented by limited practical experience in arbitration until 1968. That year I was asked to mediate my first public sector dispute. I had had no mediation or negotiation experience or credentials. It was only by frequent recesses and with phone calls to Eva Robins, one of the best known mediators in the nation, who was then working with the New York City Office of Collective Bargaining, that I was able to muddle through the dispute, which the parties fortunately settled. I've often wondered what would have happened to the parties to that dispute if Eva Robins had not been such a kind person—or if she had been out working on her own case that day.

Until 1971 there was no written description of mediation, let alone a "handbook." In 1971 William Simkin authored his *Mediation and the Dynamics of Collective Bargaining* (pp. 410, BNA, Washington, D.C.), and Walter A. Maggiolo published his *Techniques of Mediation in Labor Disputes* (pp. 192, Oceana Publications, Inc., Dobbs Ferry, N.Y.). In 1976 Eva Robins and Tia Schneider Denenberg wrote their very helpful pamphlet, *A Guide for Labor Mediators,* published by the Industrial Relations Center of the University of Hawaii. These volumes provided some guidance for new mediators, but the experience of these experts came largely from the private sector and offered only limited help to those mediators and advocates who were new to the emerging public sector.

The past decade has seen an even greater expansion of mediation in the public sector. New mediators and new labor and management advocates continue to come on the scene with little awareness of what the process calls for them to do. Despite this spread of mediation, no comprehensive volume directed at the problems of public sector mediation has appeared, either for the mediator or for the parties required to use that forum.

The shortage of written guides through the mediation process is attributable in part to the privacy of the process. Neither mediators nor the parties are anxious to have outside observers or academicians chronical their proclamations, their confidential asides, their probes, or their protests. And certainly the amount of time in mediation devoted to initial posturing and feinting would discourage even the most careful student of the negotiating process. But a more likely reason for the absence of a thorough guide through the mediation maze is the individualistic nature of the process.

Mediators, almost by definition, work alone. They develop their own techniques for handling the sequence of meetings, the presentation of positions, the secret sessions in the hallway, the wording of offers, and the other elements of the mediation process. For this reason it is difficult for any volume on mediation to present clear directions for a "traditional" or well-trod route to a mediated settlement.

This book is largely a reflection of my own experiences as an independent mediator. I have spoken with other mediators and with labor and management advocates at some length about their mediation experiences, and have sought to incorporate what they have told me into this book. But the experiences cited in this book are primarily from my own practice. Whether the incidents come from my own, or from reported experiences of others, they are but a lackluster substitute for the excitement and stimulation that comes from being a mediator in a live case.

My effort to provide as wide a range of mediation experience as possible has been aided by a recent study of techniques used by state and federal mediators undertaken by a friend and former neighbor, Deborah Kolb. Her Ph.D. thesis provides valuable insight into the differing styles used by state and federal mediators. My references to the two schools of mediators, the Orchestrators and the Dealmakers, are taken from her study.[1]

Additional input was provided by several neutrals who reviewed an early draft of the manuscript and provided comments based on their own experience as mediators. Rich Bloch, Tom Colosi, John Dorr, Bruce Fraser, Bob Stutz, and Jeffrey Tener were all most helpful in reviewing the manuscript. Laurie Thompson not only provided substantive comments but also helped immeasurably with her editing skills. I am particularly indebted to Patty Savage for her overnight typing wonders, her accuracy, and her "enthusiasm" for typing yet another draft. My thanks are due to Mary Green Miner and Don Farwell of BNA for their support from the stage of the original idea through to the finished product.

As in any other venture, the first steps of coping with the mediation process are the hardest. This book is intended to help those who are newly thrust into the mediation arena. Perhaps it will provide a useful description of the mediation process, as practiced in the labor arena, for those who seek to develop similar processes for application in other types of disputes that plague our society.

The volume first seeks to state what mediation is, how it is distinguished from the other elements of the negotiation process, and how it has evolved in the collective bargaining context. It then attempts to identify the characteristics and the qualities that competent mediators should possess.

After this description of the process and the participants, the book discusses the prerequisites for commencing mediation: the breakdown of direct negotiations, the designation of the mediator for the parties' dispute, establishing contact with the mediator, and preparing, both procedurally and substantively, for the first mediation session. It then considers the various ways of handling the initial presentation of the issues, as well as the different types of meetings with each team, with both teams, with each spokesperson, and with both spokespersons. Problems that are confronted by the parties as well as by the mediator during the course of the mediation also are considered.

---

[1] Deborah M. Kolb, *The Mediators* (Cambridge, Mass.: MIT Press, 1983).

The volume concludes with an examination of the momentum as the process nears an end, whether it be toward agreement or a breaking off of the mediation.

A final word of appreciation is due to my wife Norma and my children, Jonathan and Rachel, whose tolerance of my work habits permitted this book to be written.

TABLE OF CONTENTS

13

14

1

ABOUT MEDIATION

Hostility and conflict are pervasive in our society and our times. The search has been for voluntary systems of conflict resolution. Mediation has had expanding appeal as a fruitful means of helping disputants to reach accommodation. The past few years have seen an increasing use of mediation in a number of new areas such as in resolving landlord-tenant disputes, environmental disputes, and international disputes. Labor mediation is the predecessor of these new mediation efforts. It constitutes a successful model of dispute resolution worthy of emulation in other disciplines.

To understand the effectiveness of labor mediation, it is helpful to consider its background, the environment in which it has evolved, and its place in the continuum of collective bargaining.

Voluntary Collective Bargaining Agreements

The labor relations systems of the United States and Canada are unique. Each emphasizes voluntarism and trust. Management and the trade union that represents the majority of the employees are accepted as the two parties in interest in the work relationship. They are encouraged to work out their own contract covering wages, hours, and working conditions, as well as the duration of that contract, and they are considered liable for living up to the terms of their commitment.

In other nations the government may encourage such voluntary settlements, but if the parties are unable to reach agreement, or if the terms of the agreement are not acceptable to that government, it retains the right to mandate conditions of employment through government labor courts or through edict.

At the same time, the obligation to adhere to the terms of the collective bargaining agreement makes the procedure for securing that agreement a matter of prime importance to both parties. Because of the binding nature of their agreement, the parties must exercise extreme care in the preliminary stages of bargaining to make sure that the final agreement is acceptable, workable, and palatable to both sides. They must be satisfied that the written agreement will permit fulfillment of the promises and commitments made prior to signing.

Negotiation

The process of working out the details of these obligations is negotiation. Negotiation provides the give-and-take between the representatives designated by each side to conduct the direct discussions that will result in agreement. That agreement may come through dropping a proposal or accepting the other side's position. It may come through compromise on each of the issues until there is agreement on all the components and, thus, a final contract. It will probably come through a combination of all three. This bilateral accommodation is traditional and is repeated every year or two in every unionized enterprise, public and private, throughout the nation.

Direct negotiations between the parties frequently go smoothly, with mutual trust and accommodation to the particular needs of each side and no need for outside intervention. Such outcomes reflect a mature relationship, the acceptance of the realities of power by the parties, and the recognition that agreement is essential for the enterprise to function.

Despite the truism that ultimate agreement is inevitable in such a relationship, stumbling blocks on the way to settlement may prevent the parties from reaching agreement without outside help. One or both sides may lack experience in negotiation. They may not trust the other side or its representatives. They may have constituents with rigidly held, unrealistic expectations for a final agreement. They may be seeking something achievable but at the wrong time or in the wrong package. And they may be subject to any number of internal political problems, pressures, and obstinacies on their own or on the other side that impede effective communication, without which direct negotiation cannot proceed.

In the world outside labor-management relations, one of two parties to a dispute may compel resort to the law. Both parties then rely upon the judiciary to examine the positions and determine the outcome. But in many pure economic transactions the two parties close their deal without expectation of continuing their relationship beyond that exchange. The labor-management relationship is like a marriage in that preservation of the partnership is usually considered to be more important to both than a victory for either in their immediate dispute. Indeed, a true victory for one party is bound to produce resentment in the other party and lead to an uncomfortable contract life. On the one side, the employer recognizes that continuation of the enterprise requires employees; that it has invested time and money in training its present employees; and that productivity will be enhanced if the employees are satisfied with their benefits and persuaded that their wages, hours, and working conditions are reasonable and equitable. On the other side, the employees recognize that continuation of their employment is dependent upon the employer's willingness to continue operating the enterprise and upon their willingness to provide the requisite services. In the private sector this requires an acceptable return on the employer's investment—an adequate profit. In the public sector it requires employer or public satisfaction with performance at a cost that avoids termination or subcontracting of the service to some outside contractor using different employees.

Both participants in the negotiating process thus have an interest in reaching an amicable conclusion to their collective bargaining negotiation. The public, too, shares in that interest.

As early as 1913 the U.S. Government recognized the need to preserve bargaining relationships and established the U.S. Conciliation Service in the Department of Labor. In 1926 it established the U.S. Board of Mediation for transportation industry disputes. These agencies, which later became the Federal Mediation and Conciliation Service (FMCS) and the National Mediation Board (NMB), respectively, were dedicated to helping the parties negotiate their collective bargaining agreements. They reflected a belief that assistance from a third party sensitive to the process and to the needs and goals of the parties might help to facilitate their reaching an agreement. This, in essence, is what mediators do.

Conciliation and Mediation: Two Roles

Mediators have two separate roles, mediating and conciliating. Traditionally, the conciliator serves as a substitute for direct negotiation between the parties, while the mediator is likely to provide personal input and suggestions to bring the parties closer together. Conciliators transmit messages, offers, positions, and rejections to representatives or teams which recognize that direct dealings have been counter-productive. The animosity of the parties prevents them from dealing objectively with the substantive issues between them. The role of communicator who does not interject personal views or provide compromise alternatives has been described by Simkin:

> "Conciliation is conceived of as a mild form of interven-
> tion limited primarily to scheduling conferences, trying to
> keep disputants talking, facilitating other procedural nice-
> ties, carrying messages back and forth between the parties,
> and generally being a 'good fellow' who tries to keep
> things calm and forward looking in a tense situation."[1]

But that textbook role has changed. Present-day mediators generally take a much more active role. Beyond merely carrying messages, they seek to narrow the area in dispute between the parties. Even in their transmittal role, mediators with their terminology or their tone often color and rephrase the positions and offers of the parties. They may do this innocently or subconsciously, if only to soften the language or make a position appear more gracious and appealing to the other team. In so doing they are venturing into the area of personal intervention and into the substance of the dispute. Most mediators take this active role much further. They may suggest to one side or the other that its position should be refined or altered in an effort to make it more appealing. They may propose substitute language to increase the likelihood of acceptance. Thus, today's definition of "mediator" incorporates the function of making suggestions and recommendations to both sides, and even offering suggestions for settlement.

Although some countries still distinguish between conciliation and mediation, or indeed provide only conciliation with minimal, if any, mediation, the role of mediator in the U.S. has come to embrace both functions, and the terms are now generally used interchangeably. Some mediators may feel more comfortable restricting themselves to the role of messenger; but the parties generally expect the "neutral" to play the more active role, with the intensity of the involvement a matter of the style of the neutral, of the preference of the parties, and of the nature of the issues in dispute.

This book is concerned with the combined or expanded role, and the mediator described here will tread both paths, transmitting mes-
sages, making suggestions, and always endeavoring to bring the parties together. Sometimes, although rarely, the mediator may concentrate on inducing the parties to resume direct negotiation, with the mediator stepping out of the dispute until the parties succeed in reaching final agreement or until they send out a call for a return to mediation. But once a mediator has entered a dispute it is likely that the parties will expect continued participation until settlement is reached.

---

[1] William E. Simkin, *Mediation and the Dynamics of Collective Bargaining* (Washington, D.C.: BNA Books, 1971), pp. 25-26.

Mediation as a Substitute for Direct Negotiation

Even though mediators might seek to steer the parties back to direct negotiation across the bargaining table, their efforts to withdraw are usually rebuffed. The request that a mediator remain in a dispute does not necessarily mean that the parties are incapable of direct negotiation. More often it means that the parties find reliance on the mediator more convenient, easing as it does their burden as negotiators.

It is unfortunate when parties opt for this crutch, but that appears to be the tendency. The presence of a mediator may prevent breakdowns in communication and outbursts of hostility between the negotiators, and it may encourage concentration on the substantive issues in dispute. Certainly there are disputes where the mediator does provide suggestions that help bridge the gap between the parties' positions and in that way move the negotiations toward settlement. But when the parties retain the mediator as a convenience and as a substitute for movement and compromise, they are demonstrating their own shortcomings as negotiators. They are ceding to an outsider the responsibility for the moves they themselves should be making.

Transferring such responsibility from their own shoulders to those of the mediator may be damaging not only to the parties but to the mediator as well. Not only does it acknowledge their weakness and shortcomings as the representatives of the parties; it also tends to fortify the ego of the mediator. If both parties rely too much on the mediator for the next move, waiting to do the mediator's bidding, the result is a shifting of responsibility for the negotiations and the settlement away from those who must live with the agreement, into the hands of the outsider. It is difficult, but essential, that the mediator retain perspective. The primary function of mediation is to facilitate the parties' negotiations, not to replace them.

Mediators should not permit themselves to become decision makers. They should be careful not to dictate the terms of the agreement or the conduct of the parties in reaching it—even though the parties may seem to be thrusting that controlling role upon them. Mediators are not the most important parties at the bargaining table. They are at best observers. They are there to make sure that communications do not fail, providing a nudge when the parties earnestly seek to do it themselves but run into difficulty in advancing the negotiations to settlement.

Too active participation, too much control, and too much dictation of position convert the negotiation process to a form of arbitration. This does great disservice to the teams as well as to their constituents, who have a right to expect that their designated representatives and not an outsider will determine their terms and conditions of employment.

Private Sector Mediation

In the private sector, the requirement of negotiation in good faith under the National Labor Relations Act (NLRA) and the numerous state collective bargaining statutes have been overwhelmingly successful in stimulating the parties toward reaching their own final agreements. The availability of federal and state mediation services has helped in this effort. The Simkin estimate of upwards of 100,000 private sector collective bargaining agreements being voluntarily concluded each year, with only a tenth of these going to federal or state mediation, still seems to be the best illustration that the process has worked.

Mediation has become that essential alternative to a total breakdown in direct communication between the parties. The need for mediation may be even more pressing when a breakdown of communication has escalated to a potential strike situation. If a strike does occur, and the working relationship is disrupted with no goods produced or services rendered or compensation provided, the negotiations and the mediation must continue or at least resume after some interruption. The ultimate need for agreement remains. Negotiations, including perhaps mediation, are still a requisite, although perhaps under more trying circumstances, for the end of the strike as well as for the achieving of the ultimate agreement.

The private sector procedure for negotiations, with or without mediation and with or without a strike, has worked so well that there has been little need for emergency governmental intervention in U.S. labor relations history. The exceptions, which have involved actual or threatened interruption of airline, railroad, coal, and similar essential activities, have been so few in number as to underscore rather than detract from the exemplary role of the private sector in voluntary impasse resolution.

Public Sector Mediation

Public sector collective bargaining received its greatest impetus from President Kennedy's 1962 Executive Order 10988, recognizing the desirability of collective bargaining for federal employees. That declaration triggered the widespread extension of similar rights to state and municipal employees. With this movement came an effort to emulate the positive record of dispute settlement in the private sector by seeking to copy its negotiation pattern, including provision for resolving public sector disputes in a manner comparable to that in the private sector. Within a few years, legislation making mediation the preferred procedure for resolving public sector contract impasses had been enacted in the majority of the states that had opted for collective bargaining in the public sector.

Despite the effort to emulate private sector procedures, the political and statutory obstacles to the strike in the public sector raised a new problem. Mediation without the prospect of the strike diluted the willingness of the parties to settle at that level. Yet some fallback procedure had to be created as a public sector substitute for the strike in the event that mediation failed. The initial effort of the legislatures was to create fact-finding procedures; when those procedures did not produce the expected results, interest arbitration statutes were enacted.

In practice, mediation components have evolved in both fact-finding procedures and interest arbitration.

Mediation During Fact Finding

Legislative draftsmen believed that a formal fact-finding hearing before a neutral on issues remaining unresolved after mediation, followed by a report setting forth the neutral's recommendations for settlement, would alert the parties and the public to what an impartial person considered a reasonable solution to the impasse, and that the parties would then agree on the report and accept the recommendations. Thus, fact finding was viewed as a viable alternative to the strike.

Since fact finding is an advisory and not a binding procedure, the fact finder is under pressure to issue recommendations that will be acceptable to the parties. Otherwise, a report and recommendations favorable to one party may cause that party to become more inflexible, even though it is unable to force the other party to agree to the recommended terms. An unaccepted fact finder's report may leave the parties hanging without further recourse if interest arbitration is not available. And if interest arbitration *is* available, its outcome may be an undesirable contract.

In order to issue acceptable recommendations, in turn, the fact finder must determine the range of the parties' expectations. This often requires holding off-the-record meetings with each side to narrow the area of conflict. In these meetings the fact finder also dons the mediator's mantle to ascertain confidentially what recommendations need to be included in the report to render it acceptable to both sides and to resolve the dispute.

A fact finder may have more clout than a traditional mediator because of the threat of publicity, but to avoid rejection of his recommendations the fact finder will find it expedient to mediate just as the mediator did. Since the fact finder's report is merely advisory to the parties, fact finding with such mediatory efforts must be considered to be but another element of the voluntary process of negotiation. The need for voluntary resolution of the parties' dispute remains.

Because of the militancy of public sector unions and the inflexibility of public sector employers, the fact-finding process proved to be ineffective in many cases. This led to the exploration of binding interest arbitration as a means of achieving finality and avoiding the illegal strikes that had become more prevalent.

Mediation During Interest Arbitration

The strike substitute for at least some classes of public employees in 20 states is *interest arbitration*—final and binding arbitration of new contract terms. The element of finality is a further stimulus to the use of mediation during fact finding to encourage settlement and thereby avoid final and binding arbitration.

But mediation also occurs in interest arbitration itself, particularly where the arbitration authority is vested in a tripartite panel. Many interest arbitrators, sensitive to the frustration or hostility of the parties, or to the possibility that an unacceptable award may trigger a strike, tend to mediate in an effort to determine what elements are necessary to reduce the conflict between the parties.

A variant of the process that has gained widening acceptability is the med-arb process pioneered by Sam and John Kagel, of San Francisco. In med-arb the parties select the neutral of their choice, who seeks to work out a settlement using the conventional techniques of mediation. If the neutral is unsuccessful in mediating a settlement, he dons his arbitrator's hat and issues a decision that the parties have agreed to accept as final and binding.

Even where binding interest arbitration is use, it is desirable to have a result the parties have helped to reach—one they find tolerable even if they do not welcome it. To achieve an element of voluntarism, even if it is realized tardily in the form of amendments to an arbitrator's interest award, requires that the lines of communications between the parties be kept open and that helpful suggestions on substantive issues be provided to them. Mediation can accomplish this.

---------------------------------- New Fields of Mediation ----------------------------------

The expansion of mediation into the public sector demonstrates its appeal to opposing parties as a practical device for resolving labor relations disputes. The spread of public sector collective bargaining statutes into the majority of states has, in turn, created a great demand for mediators. Whether they work at the mediation step, or mediate as an adjunct to their fact-finding responsibilities, or perhaps in connection with their duties as interest arbitrators, mediators are recognized for the crucial role they play in labor dispute settlement.

The mediatory role is not a transitory one. If the parties believe that the process has helped them to settle, they will return to mediation for help in resolving subsequent disputes. Once tried, mediation continues to be used and to spread geographically to those states with new collective bargaining laws. It is used even in states without statutes, where the parties themselves often negotiate impasse procedures involving mediation.

At the same time, the public has become increasingly aware of the role of mediation in deterring litigation and in resolving disputes that might otherwise result in disruption of public service and other public inconvenience. This, in turn, has stimulated interest in applying the mediation process to other types of disputes—environmental disputes, police–community disputes, warranty disputes, divorce and property settlements, and the like.

In the other types of conflict the traditions, language, impact, format, responsibility, numbers, roles, and relationships of the participants, as well as the role of a written document, may all be quite different from those in labor-management disputes. Yet there may be elements that are alike and perhaps pertinent and adaptable or transferable. The role of the mediator as intervener, communicator, facilitator, and legitimizer of the negotiating process; the need for continuing acceptability; the handling of obstacles; the development of priorities for attacking the outstanding issues; the exchanges between representatives; the effectiveness of joint or separate sessions with leaders and teams—the whole range of techniques employed by labor-management mediators may have surprising relevance and potential for those endeavoring to resolve the diverse new areas of community and interpersonal disputes.

Yet there is no model format for a labor mediation. There is not even a typical mediation. Each case is unique. Thus it is difficult to offer a systematic exposition of the process. In addition to the procedural substantive variations that obviously make each case different and account for the differences in mediator style, there are variations in how the parties view and participate in the process and how they deal with the mediator. Variables in the mediation process include whether the participants are experienced or naive, whether they are represented by consultants or attorneys, whether the relationship is new or one that is long established, whether the dispute is in the public focus, and whether the parties really wish to resolve their dispute. Add to these variables the differences in mediator backgrounds, techniques, personalities, and experiences, and in the trust the parties place in the mediator, and it becomes evident that there can be no formulation of the ideal mediation procedure.

Even though the process is a fluid one, without fixed rules or procedures, and one in which different mediators utilize different techniques in attempting to resolve disputes, both the mediator and the disputing parties can benefit from a broader understanding of how the process works. So too can the public, which is, after all, the ultimate beneficiary of all procedures for conflict resolution.

Public Responsibility

Clearly the creation of the two federal mediation agencies, the Federal Mediation and Conciliation Service and the National Mediation Board, and the numerous state mediation agencies reflects a public policy endorsing the function and use of mediation. It is often the parties' recognition of its role in our national labor policy that opens the door for a mediator to join their negotiations.

The question naturally arises whether the mediator's primary duty is to serve the public interest or to assist the parties. This is particularly pertinent when one considers that the "government" that may provide the mediator in a public sector dispute is also the employer. The issue of divided loyalties is obvious.

A touchstone of the public and statutory endorsement of the mediation process is that the public interest lies only in facilitating the parties' negotiations. To this end the emphasis has always been to provide mediators to help the parties with their dispute rather than to designate agents charged with imposing a governmental or public position upon the parties. While the mediator may be cloaked in statutory authority, the negotiating process is very much the parties' own. The mediator's function is to facilitate the parties' reaching of their own settlement goals, not to direct them toward the mediator's set of goals. For if the latter were to occur, the parties would simply discard the mediator and proceed on their own, or jointly select another mediator more in sympathy with their view of the dispute.

Nonetheless, mediators may express their views to the parties on issues of public policy when faced with the prospect of an illegal provision in the agreement. Most mediators in such cases would advise the parties of the potential illegality and of the potential consequences of their proposed actions. Yet it would be inconsistent with their role, and indeed their authority, for them to do more. The parties must have the authority to conclude their own agreement. As in the case of a mediator embracing an objectionable policy, the parties after receiving the mediator's opinion could, if bent on reaching their illegal goal, exclude the mediator from their sessions and proceed on their own. Recognizing this fact, mediators tend to limit any involvement in public policy issues to advising the parties of their personal opinions. In any case they may not have sufficient knowledge of the proposals or of the applicable law even to develop a credible personal opinion as to the legality of a proposal.

A mediator claiming to represent the public interest becomes an advocate and thereby abdicates his neutral posture. Such a mediator becomes no different from any of the other advocates in the room. The great strength of the labor-management mediation system is the insistence on the neutrality of the mediator, who must be unencumbered. A problem with importing mediation into other types of disputes is that those who would prescribe mediation for such conflicts become advocates of mediation and thus unacceptable to the adversaries who need it most.

Summary

Mediation, then, is but one phase of the negotiation process. It is a process to which the parties resort because they have failed to communicate or to reach a substantive accommodation on the issues facing them. The mediator provided by a federal or state agency or designated by the parties is a person whose authority and responsibility are derived from the parties themselves.

Through a variety of techniques and approaches that have come to be accepted by the labor-management community as the appropriate practice of mediation, the mediator seeks to bring the parties together. He may participate in negotiations until agreement is reached; alternatively—and preferably—he may withdraw from time to time as the parties resolve temporary impediments, permitting them to resume direct negotiations with no outside help.

The tradition of providing assistance only to parties desiring it, and the generally positive results that have become the hallmark of labor-management mediation, have inspired interest in mediation as a valuable tool for helping to resolve other types of disputes that increasingly trouble our society. Much of its success in the labor-management sphere is due to the unique nature of the statutory ongoing, bipartisan labor-management relationship in the context of its enforceable written agreements. Yet there may be elements of mediation that have application to other fields, and indeed there are lessons to be learned by labor-management mediators and advocates themselves from such application.

2

THE NEED FOR MEDIATORS

With the expanding use of mediation, more and more people appear interested in undertaking mediation careers. Some want to mediate as a full-time occupation. Some see mediation as a step to a career in arbitration. Some view mediation as a capstone to careers as advocates for labor and management. Despite the conviction and dedication of these would-be mediators, success as a mediator is not predictable. It is something over which the mediator may have little, if any, control.

This chapter explores the avenues by which people have entered the mediation profession, and then looks at the continuing need for proficient mediators.

Selection and Training of Private Sector Mediators

Prior to the advent of collective bargaining in the public sector all but a handful of full-time mediators were employed by the Federal Mediation and Conciliation Service, which restricted itself largely to private sector disputes; the National Mediation Board, which handled only disputes in the transportation industry; and the few state mediation agencies, which were limited to mediating disputes involving intrastate private sector employers. These original private sector mediation facilities have continued to provide mediation services in their respective arenas.

FMCS Mediators

One might expect the FMCS mediators to have come from lifetimes of service as neutrals. But the agency's roster shows that only a third had backgrounds as neutrals or as academics. Two thirds of the FMCS mediators came from careers in either management or trade unions.

It would further seem that years of representing only one side would brand former personnel directors, company vice presidents, union business agents, and international representatives as partisans, totally unacceptable to the side they had spent their lives opposing. Yet the evidence shows that the parties prefer mediators who have had real-life negotiating experience. Work as partisans did not necessarily eradicate their sense of fairness and justice, or their objectivity.

The FMCS has tended to hire as mediators advocates who were respected and often recommended by their counterparts. Their years of experience at the negotiating table and in contract administration instilled in them a facility in resolving disputes for which no amount of classroom training or book learning could substitute. They were familiar with the internal political problems that tend to plague unions and managements, and with the prevailing labor-management customs and practices in their own and perhaps other industries. They had observed and been party to the mediation process and the often tedious efforts to exact concessions, secure altered proposals and compromises, hold caucuses, entreat, cajole, and pressure the parties toward settlement.

But even though they participated in mediation, these former advocates were not experienced in functioning as neutrals. They, as well as the minority of new mediators without advocacy experience, needed to be trained in the special skills of a mediator.

FMCS Training

The FMCS was the first to develop mediation training programs to help fill this need, and such training has continued to be an important FMCS service. The FMCS has traditionally relied on simulated mediation sessions and now uses video taping as well. In the simulated sessions, trainees serve as advocates and as mediators, with experienced mediators providing critiques. Workshops are also held on the practices and tradition of mediation, on industrial, economic, and regional labor relations trends, and on prevailing standards for settlements in various industries. In addition, mediator trainees spend an extended period in an apprentice type of relationship in which they observe and discuss the techniques and approaches actually used by experienced mediators. The trainee thereby gains valuable insights from the mentor on what to do and, perhaps more important, what *not* to do. Eventually the trainee assumes a more active role in the mediation process, being given responsibility for one or two ancillary issues until he demonstrates the ability to function independently.

The FMCS also provides refresher training through conferences, seminars, and programs in which staff mediators exchange experiences, learn of current labor relations problems, and discuss new techniques of dispute settlement.

State Agency Training

In the state agencies employing staff mediators, the selection of mediators resembles the practice at the federal level. There, too, the majority of those selected appear to have had advocacy experience, with the minority coming from neutral or academic backgrounds.

Because of the limited size of state mediation staffs, time pressures, and limited resources, less classroom training is provided than at the federal level. Less emphasis is placed by the state agencies on training in general, although trainees are given some apprenticeship training in the company of more experienced staff mediators.

Many of the state agencies are unable to provide refresher training, although there have been some staff seminars and some regional efforts at multistate training through a series of state agency consortiums. These consortiums provide discussion of legal and other developments in areas with which a mediator must be familiar, such as discrimination, maternity leave, Employee Retirement Income Security Act (ERISA), insurance liability, teacher tenure rules, local budgeting, and state funding.

State consortiums also may use video tapes as a training aid. For example, an audience of mediators may watch taped sequences of two advocates arguing their respective positions on a particular issue. An instructor then guides the mediators in a discussion of how they would respond to the situation just presented and to related problems. Such discussions not only acquaint the mediators with problems they may confront but also provide the reassurance that other mediators may be similarly perplexed by such issues. Most important, the format encourages discussion of alternative ways of overcoming difficulties. Since mediators work alone, and cannot discuss tactics as problems arise, the opportunity for the exchange of ideas with other mediators and for reevaluating customary practices is of signal benefit.

Two national professional organizations to which many agencies and mediators belong and which also provide training opportunities in mediation techniques at their national and regional meetings are the Association of Labor Relations Agencies and the Society of Professionals in Dispute Resolution.

The New Demand for Public Sector Mediators

As noted in Chapter 1, the adoption of collective bargaining statutes for public employees in the majority of states since the mid 1960s has led to the general acceptance of mediation in the public sector. In industrial states, the number of public sector bargaining units may equal or exceed the number of private sector industrial enterprises. Public sector operations are likely to have similar or identical contract expiration and funding dates, a condition leading to a seasonal rash of negotiations. Although there is great variation in procedures for carrying on these negotiations, the significant common thread is the provision for mediation to assist the parties toward settlement prior to fact finding, arbitration, or the exercise of any right to strike.

The rapid spread of state statutes has also led to the introduction of and reliance on the process in states without legislation. Enlightened parties in a number of communities have voluntarily adopted mediation as a means of resolving disputes over contract renegotiation. In most of these communities the municipality or the school authority has provided in its collective bargaining agreements for mediation of any remaining issues if direct negotiations do not produce a settlement by the deadline date. In the event of impasse they conform to their previously negotiated procedures for the selection of a mediator, who is usually to be designated through the facilities of the American Arbitration Association if the parties themselves are unable to agree upon a mediator. The mediation agreement may go into such details as the scheduling and location of sessions, the number of participants to be allowed each team, the issues subject to or excluded from mediation, the basis for determining the compensation of the mediator, and the like. In some cases the parties' agreement goes on to provide for fact finding and in rare instances even interest arbitration.

In the "new" public sector bargaining relationships, initial expectations, fiscal restraints, inexperience, political problems on both sides, and the continuing prospect of the strike combine to make the need for mediators far more acute than it has been in the more experienced private sector. This burgeoning demand for public sector mediation has frequently overwhelmed state mediation agencies staffed to handle only the limited number of private sector cases over which the FMCS does not assert jurisdiction. Many state agencies have suffered from budget inadequacies and from civil service and seniority limitations placed upon their personnel, and have not been able to meet the demand for proficient mediators resulting from the expansion of mediation into the public sector.

As difficult as the problem in the industrialized states has been, it has been even greater in the primarily rural and agricultural states, which had not previously developed mediation agencies because of the lack of a substantial private sector industrial economy. Lacking private sector agency staff to aid them in developing and staffing public sector agencies, these states have often been unable to meet the heavy new demand for mediation. The result has been a heavy burden placed on their new agencies and on any available mediators, regardless of their training or their experience.

Deadlines and Seasonality

There is another factor, inherent in public sector mediation, that militates against the goal of full-time staffing. Negotiations, in the private sector, tend to occur throughout the year, permitting the employment of a fixed number of full-time mediators who expect year-round work. But public sector mediation occurs in cycles: One of these is determined by annual budgets; with funding based on annual appropriations by state or local legislative bodies, the budget deadline creates a deadline for negotiations. If agreement for compensation is not reached by that deadline, wage increases may go unfunded.

Another cycle is the work calendar of the services involved. The pressure of securing an agreement covering teachers before the start of school is felt on both sides and creates a very real deadline for negotiations to be concluded, with mediation if required. For garbage collectors a summer contract deadline creates far greater public pressure for settlement, again with mediation if called for, than one during the winter. The opposite is the case for licensed boiler room employees.

These calendar deadlines may not be reached. Employers may be able to exercise sufficient persuasion, or power, to move the deadlines to less threatening dates. But powerful unions are capable of extending negotiations to more favorable deadlines, as when a town's lifeguards push their contract deadline from winter into the hot summer weather.

In some states the mix of contract deadlines permits fairly steady utilization of mediator skills throughout the year. In other states all bargaining units may adhere to the same deadline, limiting the demand for mediators to one season. The latter group includes states that fix the period for negotiation, mediation, fact finding, and interest arbitration by statute; in general, the number of mediators available during that period has been insufficient.

Ad Hoc Mediators

The sharply increasing but often seasonal need for mediators has led to the emergence of a new breed of neutrals: ad hoc mediators. They include prior advocates, arbitrator-mediators, arbitrators without prior mediation experience, and a fourth group, heretofore lacking any previous labor-management experience.

Prior Advocates

Some of the mediators, like those with prior advocacy experience who have traditionally worked as private sector mediators, are retired labor and management advocates who have persuaded the designating agencies of their acceptability and qualifications. Many of these have proved to be effective and are used repeatedly by designating agencies and the parties who select mediators directly. Their experience usually far exceeds that possessed by the parties on either side, and has made them welcome as independent, forthright educators in the techniques of negotiation as well as effective mediators. The cyclical nature of public sector mediation work and the ancillary retirement income it provides have made for comfortable careers. Some of this group, however, although appearing qualified, have not been well received by the parties because of suspicions about their prior affiliations and present loyalty. This has limited their use.

Arbitrator-Mediators

Arbitrators who have previously worked as mediators, and perhaps even as partisans before that, constitute a second group that has helped meet the increasing demand for mediators. This group also includes a few retired private sector mediators who have come back to active work as public sector mediators.

The services of this group have been greatly in demand because of their prior experience in the mediation field. They have brought a higher level of professionalism to the state agencies, in a sense legitimizing the rosters of the neutrals. They possess the level of expertise necessary to help the parties reach settlement in the most difficult cases, and they also provide valuable guidance to the newer entrants into the field.

But those in this group are likely to have gruelling schedules. Evening and weekend mediation meetings are required when public sector employers are unwilling or unable to release negotiating teams during "normal working hours." Night travel to the sessions in small communities can be a burden, particularly for the older mediators. Added to this is the uncertainty of the duration of mediations between inexperienced parties facing no strike deadline. The result is that members of this group frequently opt to confine their availability to the more remunerative, more convenient, and usually better presented arbitration cases to which they can gain ready access during "normal working hours." They may do some mediation, but they often impose restrictions as to location, duration, type of dispute, and number of cases they will accept.

Arbitrators Turned Mediators

A third group that has sought to fill the vacuum consists of those without prior mediation or negotiation experience. They tend to be a larger group, some of whom are arbitrators who have come into the practice of mediation without prior service as advocates for either side. Some have come into practice through apprenticeships in steel and autos; while they were accepted and relatively experienced as arbitrators, most lacked the experience of personal involvement in negotiations or mediation. Their forte generally has been in contract interpretation and in the exercise of their authority as decision makers, their backgrounds and strengths often presenting the very antithesis of the humility and surrender of authority usually attributed to mediators. Yet they, too, entered the fray, learning to mediate by doing it. Some became competent mediators; others returned to arbitration.

The Neophytes

Another group of inexperienced new mediators are those who have entered mediation practice without having any previous relations as negotiators, arbitrators, or mediators. These have been academicians teaching labor relations, law, economics, or public administration, and a few of their former students, who had not yet had any practical on-the-job experience in the dispute-settlement arena in negotiations, in arbitration, or in mediation. Members of this group tend to appear in geographical areas lacking mediators from any of the three other groups. They are often called upon to mediate when the pressure of a pending dispute forces the designating agency or the parties themselves to select someone to calm the waters, deter press criticism, and provide some semblance of expertise in labor-management relations. Despite their geographic isolation from the more experienced practicing neutrals, their lack of experience in the trenches, and the lack of any real guidance as to how to mediate, many of this group have succeeded and now constitute a sizable portion of current public sector mediators. They have availability, flexibility of schedule, and empathy with parties who, like themselves, are inexperienced in the process. In addition, in many cases they have the substantive knowledge of many of the classification and administrative matters of which private sector arbitrators may know little. Many have been academically trained in disciplines that are directly related to the issues they may deal with as mediators: public administration, education, finance, public law. They can therefore often provide greater guidance to the parties about the pitfalls of their proposals and positions than could the intervening arbitrator or even the private sector mediator who is new to the public sector.

All four groups of "ad hoc" mediators have to varying degrees come to the rescue of public sector parties in need of mediators. They have been able to meet the seasonal needs; they have achieved enough respect and acceptability to merit their use in subsequent disputes in the same and other districts; they have built substantial reputations as dispute settlers which has led to their being used repeatedly, contributing to their professionalism and thus building their expertise. They have made a substantial contribution to the widespread use of public sector mediation.

Mediator Turnover

The veteran mediators with prior mediation and negotiation experience are getting old. As discussed above, they are reluctant to work the erratic schedules, far from home. In addition, private sector arbitrators doing public sector mediation find it difficult to fit mediation work into their arbitration schedules, which are often fixed months in advance. It may be impossible to rearrange schedules to make an immediate date to mediate, and if a date is available the mediation may nonetheless require still further schedule readjustments until settlement is achieved.

Since the absence of a strike deadline in the public sector creates a tendency for mediation to drag on far longer than it would in the private sector, some arbitrators who seek mediation work block out two or three consecutive days every month or two to be held in reserve for such cases. It may also be the reason why some arbitrators mediate only outside their home state. Their scheduled departure date and the extra transportation cost of a return create a practical and costly deadline for the parties. It imposes a subtle pressure to settle that the parties might not feel with their local mediators, who are perpetually available at no additional travel cost. As one representative said to me during a mediation far from home, "We pay all that money to an experienced mediator as well as to our attorney. All the time the clock is running. If both say we should change our position, it is silly to throw all that money away to resist and rely on our inexperienced viewpoint. I guess we should offer to compromise."

Even the "neophyte" mediators who lack prior labor or management experience tend eventually to have less time for the work. Those who have been successful at public sector mediation find themselves asked to serve as arbitrators in public sector and even private sector grievance resolution. And since grievance arbitration work may become more financially rewarding with a far more comfortable work schedule, those in this group, too, tend to become less readily available for mediation.

Thus, although the influx of new people into public sector mediation work over the past decade has been substantial, the pressures of the work and the lure of arbitration have tended to cut back on when and where they will be willing to mediate. This reduced availability comes at a time when the processes of collective bargaining and impasse resolution are continuing to expand to new communities, when economic pressures are making negotiations more difficult, and when individual union member militancy is forcing more tenacious positions in the mediation process.

Summary

The expanding demand for mediators at a time when those with years of experience as negotiators, mediators, and even arbitrators are less willing to make themselves available for mediation raises an important question about qualifications. It would be desirable to find and provide to the parties new mediators in the old mold—but they just aren't available. The number of competent ad hoc mediators is small compared to the number who would like to do the work or who hold themselves out as mediators. Indeed, in the general absence of training or certification programs, anyone can proclaim himself a mediator.

Despite the laudable efforts of most state agencies to filter out the less competent, in the absence of any other training source the parties themselves tend to become the trainers and certifiers of the new mediators. They provide mediator recruits with what is probably the best substitute for the years of advocacy experience enjoyed by the older generation of private sector mediators. In short, they provide the new mediators with both initial and growing experiences. Although the risk of fatalities may be greater for naive, boot-strapping mediators dealing with naive, inexperienced parties, the survivors will bring to their future cases the battle scars necessary to establish their qualifications.

3
QUALIFICATIONS OF MEDIATORS

The success of mediation as a reliable instrument for assisting disputants to resolve their differences is dependent on the quality of the mediators.

Art or Trade

The spreading interest in mediation has raised anew the question of whether mediation is an art or a trade. Is it an innate skill or one that can be learned?

Before I began to mediate in the early days of public sector collective bargaining, my perception as an arbitrator was that mediation was indeed an art. It was practiced by federal magicians who, despite prior partisan affiliation, were able to lure warring parties into settling their differences.

That is probably a valid appraisal for the legendary mediators who were able to react to repeated conflict and confrontation with innovation and insight born of their years of advocacy and their innate sense of equity and fairness. It is probably equally applicable today when applied to the "best" mediators. But the spread of mediation to the public sector and to so many new geographical areas has created a demand that unquestionably exceeds the supply of top-flight mediators. The success of the newer, less well-grounded mediators convinces me that there is room in the field for those who are willing and eager to learn the process. They may never have the artistic touch of the old timers, but they meet the parties' needs and they make up the main corps of present-day mediators.

Mediation is a learnable trade. Few of the new mediators have undergone much formal training; the majority have trained themselves through on-the-job trial and error, occasionally at the expense of their clients. This process, together with the encouragement of parties and public, has probably transformed what was indeed originally an art into what more closely resembles a trade. The artisans, however, are still at work, the parties still recognize their handiwork, and the skills of the expert mediator will continue to set the standard which the tradesmen should seek to emulate.

22

As to whether the practice of mediation in new fields beyond labor-management relations is art or trade, the answer seems clear that art still prevails. Mediators of family, environmental, business, waste disposal, and other disputes must be far more innovative than the labor relations mediator ordinarily needs to be. They don't merely respond to a request for mediation between two well-established adversaries who may know the procedures and techniques better than the mediator. They must, in these newer areas of mediation, guide the adversaries, regardless of the number, into acceptance of the concept of mediation. They must guide them into the development of rules and guidelines for administering the process. And they must guide them into the acceptance of a mutually satisfactory basis for settlement, without any of the norms that labor-management mediators now accept and embrace.

If these innovative artisans are successful, as were the early pioneers of labor-management mediation, in gaining acceptance of the process, mediation in these new areas may some day become comparably "institutionalized." The tradesmen can then enter the fray and assure that the resulting systems are put to good work—for society's benefit.

The challenge today in labor-management mediation is to attract into the trade those who have the innate skills to permit their rise above tradesman status to the artisan level. The absence of any formal training or certification program for mediators makes it more difficult for mediators to rise to that level. But it is also a strength, in that it underscores the voluntary nature of the process, the responsibility of the disputants to work with and rely upon mediators of their choice, and the need for mediators to practice the craft in order to master it. The obligation of those who believe in mediation and endorse its survival is to encourage those who have the threshold qualifications and to deter those who would embrace it as merely a trade.

Qualifications for Entry

What are the appropriate qualifications that one should possess in seeking to gain acceptability as a mediator? What factors should the state agency or the parties look for in selecting a mediator whom they have never used before?

Simkin, in a humorous vein, identified 10 qualities that the "ideal" mediator should possess:

1. the patience of Job;
2. the sincerity and bulldog characteristics of the English;
3. the wit of the Irish;

4. the physical endurance of the marathon runner;
5. the broken field dodging abilities of a halfback;
6. the guile of Machiavelli;
7. the personality probing skills of a good psychiatrist;
8. the confidence retaining characteristics of a mute;
9. the hide of a rhinoceros;
10. the wisdom of Solomon.[2]

The personal characteristics that I think are important are diverse and may appear contradictory. But different situations call for the application of different skills. What is needed is the ability to apply the right skill at the right juncture. Here is what one should look for in a mediator:

Humility

Mediators should be humble, but certainly not obsequious. They should respect the fact that the dispute and the negotiating process belong to the parties. The mediator is there to help the parties reach their own agreement; he is not there to impose the settlement that he thinks will best serve the parties. Mediators are not to be confused with arbitrators called upon to decide; rather, they are there to use their powers of persuasion to bring the parties' positions closer together. One task of the mediator is to suggest alternatives to the parties to help narrow their differences. But the mediator who is too forward in that regard may be viewed by one of the parties as too aggressive. Such conduct might be seen as reflecting a tilt toward the position of one of the parties or the mediator's own prejudices. In either case the credibility and tenure of the mediator might well be jeopardized. The autocrat at the mediation table is not likely to inspire trust and confidence. Humility more frequently will. The mediator should be content to do only what is necessary to keep the parties working jointly toward *their* settlement.

Lack of humility can prove to be a mediator's Achilles' heel. Those who have been arbitrators, or even university professors, are used to being in command and may find it difficult to play the role of bystander while the parties work things out on their own. Yet the desire to have the parties agree on the neutral's own "best" solution may prove fatal if discerned by the parties. The mediator's most difficult task—but one that experienced practitioners perceive as an essential one—is to get the parties back to direct negotiations as often as possible so that the mediator's input is *not* needed. The process does, after all, belong to the parties.

---

[2] William E. Simkin, *Mediation and the Dynamics of Collective Bargaining* (Washington, D.C.: BNA Books, 1971), p. 53.

Patience

Another valuable trait, akin to humility, is patience. The parties have to move through the process at their own pace. It is far better that they take somewhat more time to reach agreement than be pushed into the same agreement too quickly. If pushed, they may spend the contract term suspecting they were "taken" and exploiting the grievance procedure in an effort to achieve what they think they could have obtained by more thorough discussion and exploration during negotiations. It is only natural for a mediator who knows "in his bones" that a settlement has to come out at "X" or that a particular proposal will never be accepted by the other side to try to nudge the recalcitrant party in order to avoid wasting time. It is also natural for a mediator who has allocated a fixed period of time to a case to seek to bring an issue to a head even though one party may still be discussing it in caucus. It is also particularly annoying to a mediator to have one party insist on prolonging the mediation when the mediator knows the chances for any change in position are nil.

But in all these circumstances a precipitous move or premature interjection by the mediator might just be enough to keep the delaying party from reaching the mediator's "X," or even from withdrawing the offending proposal. It might magnify the importance of a position that otherwise would have washed away.

The problem is more obvious in the public sector than in the private sector. Patience is more likely to wear thin in a public sector mediation because of the absence of a strike or other meaningful deadline to force the parties to bargain seriously and give ground. Yet mediators accept that impediment when they take public sector cases. They could decline the cases, or take them with the specification that they would withdraw at a certain point. But unless there is some means of forestalling the delays of one or both sides, mediators may jeopardize any progress the parties may be making as well as their own acceptability if they are perceived as pushing one or both parties out of impatience or for reasons of their own convenience.

Another reason for exercising patience is that labor-management impasses ultimately are broken with or without the assistance of mediators. If they are patient and do not interfere too much, mediators can rightfully claim a share of the credit for the ultimate settlement—if only because they stayed out of the parties' way.

There are times, it is true, where pressures and interventions are crucial tools of the mediator, but the use of such tools should be well thought out and not motivated by pique or impatience. The mediator must be a patient listener; he must not hog the process and must be mindful of the fact that it is the parties' process and to the extent possible must be orchestrated by their timetable.

Sensitivity

Mediators must be sensitive. The parties are usually deeply committed to their proposals and positions, which have been arrived at through a long process of solicitation and selection. The proposals that have survived this winnowing process to come before the mediator have assumed a life of their own. The parties ardently believe in them. The mediator cannot treat them with disdain or ungraciously belittle them, or even suggest they be modified without giving a real jolt to their sponsors. Mediators must recognize this possessiveness and be sensitive to the importance each position has assumed. Such sensitivity is essential if there is to be any effective effort toward persuading a party to modify a position or withdraw from it. It should be demonstrated by never making adverse or critical comments about the individuals on either team, or in faulting or blaming anyone for any dilemma or problem. Such comments rapidly get back to the person at whom they are directed, to the disadvantage of the mediator as well as the process.

Sensitivity must also be employed when framing one party's negative response to the other side's unacceptable proposal. Mediators should be able to soften a "tell them to go to hell" into language that will not result in confrontation or rigidity. They should be able to phrase responses from the opposing team so that doors remain open to further exchanges on the subject in question.

Sense of Timing

Akin to sensitivity is a good sense of timing. Mediators can make or break a session by an ill-timed comment or suggestion and must learn to sense the best and worst times to do or say things. A given proposal made at point X in a session may be met with wrath, yet if offered in exactly the same form 10 minutes later may be viewed as salvation. An extended caucus by one side will be viewed as conveying a message to the other side that is quite different from that conveyed by a short caucus. The mediator, as the orchestrator, may contribute mightily by the way in which he times such sessions, breaks, proposals, and caucuses with each side or jointly. He must know when to bring the parties together and when to keep them apart, when to talk to each team, and when to speak privately to one or both spokespersons.

Tolerance

Mediators must be personally thick-skinned while retaining their sensitivity toward the parties' needs. If the parties are in separate locations and the mediator is the only link between them, there is no one else against whom frustrations and anger can be vented. Mediators often become the recipients of pent-up hostility. Abuse and expressions of frustration are usually not intended personally and should not be so taken. The attacker will usually recognize that such displays of temper against the mediators are misplaced, and apologies are likely to be forthcoming. But even if they are not offered, the mediator must recognize that it is what is being relayed rather than the mediators' role that is the cause of the outrage.

There may, of course, be situations in which it is difficult for the mediators to shrug off such attacks—where, for example, it was the mediator who proposed a modification of position or where the mediator has inadequately or inaccurately relayed a position. Nevertheless, the mediator should not take a rebuff to heart. The process requires alternative proposals, and it is the mediator's job to provide them. If rebuffed, try again; mediators should not bind themselves to positions any more than should the parties. A substantial part of the mediator's role entails negotiating with each side toward a change in position. If what the mediator suggests in such negotiations is rejected, it should be considered merely a prelude to a more acceptable alternative. Egos may be bruised under such pressures, but the focus on issue rather than position must prevail, with egos being sacrificed.

The situation is somewhat different where there has been faulty relaying of messages by the mediator, a serious error indeed. Such failings are distressing—but they do happen. They are a jolt to one's sense of professionalism, but they should be no more than a warning to be more thorough or accurate in future relays. If the mediator has been forthright, honest, humble, and sensitive to the parties' needs, the teams usually will overlook the mistake and go about their business. It is at this point that the personal credibility and trust the mediator has been building with the teams pays off. There are times, however, when an error may be fatal, leading one or both parties to request the mediator's withdrawal. That can bruise the ego, too, but a clever though battered mediator can always rationalize that it was the message rather than the messenger that upset the parties. Of all the contributions that mediators may make to the process of dispute settlement—as interveners, facilitators, and legitimizers—none may be as important as being the scapegoat.

Humor

A good sense of humor is a great asset to a mediator. Negotiations are not necessarily fun, but when parties are deeply immersed in the process a touch of levity from time to time may be just what is needed to break tensions, put positions in a different perspective, or enhance confidence in the neutrals. But just as newer mediators may tend to pontificate, mediators of the old school may tend to rely excessively on war stories. The parties don't want, and usually won't tolerate, a buffoon as their mediator. Yet for the professional representatives, who tend to be more objective about their client's proposals, a separation of issues from participants is important, and a good sense of humor on the part of the mediator can be helpful as a means of reducing tensions.

The use of humor also helps to separate mediators from too close an identification with either side. Although they try to be equally accessible to the parties as essential to maintaining their acceptability, there are occasions when suspicion is bound to arise. This may occur when they spend what seems to be an inordinate amount of time with one of the other parties, or when they relay a message of rejection. In such circumstances, a comment such as "Gosh, did they take me over the coals," or "I thought I'd give you lots of time to reexamine your position," or "Well, that didn't fly, let's try something else," may be enough to break the tension and return the focus to the issues.

Ability to Innovate

Mediators must be innovative. They must be able not only to convey messages and attitudes accurately but also to sense areas of resistance and of pliability and to reshape the proposals or arguments to make them more palatable to the opposing party. Mediators must be accomplished in rephrasing statements and subtly suggesting changes in position. In doing this, knowledge of prevailing practices and contract provisions in the area or the classification may enable them to pick helpful ideas from one or a number of contracts. This enables them to propose minor adjustments in positions to make them more acceptable and to provide a basis for continued progress toward settlement.

The art of subtle innovation is a far cry from the "I know better" or "listen to me" school. It requires planting the seed in such a manner that the parties can take credit for the breakthrough. The effective and secure mediators are the ones who take satisfaction from the parties' sense of accomplishment without feeling the need to proclaim their role in that change.

Collective Bargaining Expertise

The foregoing list of attributes is not unique to people who proclaim themselves to be mediators; indeed, they are characteristics that many in the population possess. Many who have served in a mediatory role in other kinds of human interaction, or who have been proclaimed for their ability to smooth ruffled feathers, believe that their demonstrated success as problem solvers in other fields constitutes qualification for success as a mediator in labor-management relations. But while those attributes of personality are necessary, something more is required, namely collective bargaining expertise. It is not readily taught nor is it readily acquired from books. However, with persistence it can be acquired through observation and participation in mediation sessions.

Mediators must know how parties agree to, adhere to, and implement collective bargaining agreements. They must share the parties' commitment to the dispute settlement process and their commitment to living with each other. If one party is lacking in experience, the mediator must alert it to those commitments. Familiarity with subjects such as union recognition, exclusivity, management rights, seniority, and grievance procedures comes from living under other collective bargaining agreements, from processing grievances, and from years of experience in reading and administering the labor agreement. It comes from knowing about other communities and other settlements. It comes from familiarity with budget construction and from understanding economic data.

Although some of the necessary knowledge can be acquired by academic studies and on-site observation—indeed, most mediators' skill derives at least in part from on-the-job training—such a process is far more time-consuming, less intensive, and less dynamic than being in the trenches as an advocate.

Analytical Ability

Mediators must have analytical powers. Comfort with and prior experience in the negotiating process and with the collective bargaining agreement endows mediators with the resources necessary to help the parties understand the implications of their positions and where alternative routes might lead. Every dispute is different and the issues are always new, but they do not arise in a vacuum. Prior experience with similar problems—whether as mediator or advocate or arbitrator—permits the mediator to analyze the problem, cull out the troublesome aspects, separate what is acceptable and undisputed from the hard core issues, and decide whether to start with the small issues or difficult ones.

In the public sector, where external law and governmental rules and regulations play a major role, such analytical powers permit review of proposals in the context of the permissible, and permit adaptations to achieve the doable. There is no ready guidebook on how to transform a firm position into a stance that will be more appealing to the other side, but that is a skill which, honed in a collective bargaining background, is essential for a good mediator.

Conceptualizing Ability

Mediators must be good conceptualizers. This skill, too, is in part a product of experience. Knowing what has been tried unsuccessfully in the past is a prerequisite for fashioning alternatives that are acceptable in the present context. Between positions of the parties there usually are myriad alternative possibilities. The most effective mediators are those who can peel off layers of the parties' positions to find what is mutually tolerable. Knowing what is practicable and realistic is essential to effective mediation. The mediator must be able to rephrase statements and demands in a way that will be acceptable to their sponsors yet non-threatening to the recipients.

Impartiality

Finally, mediators must be impartial. They must build and maintain credibility with both parties. This doesn't mean they must be spineless. They must be able to be critical, forceful, and outspoken at the same time that they are seeking voluntary movement toward settlement. Since the perception of impartiality is as important as impartiality itself, they must be viewed by the parties as committed to getting a settlement rather than committed to either party. They must continue to be viewed as acceptable at the same time they are in effect destroying the very fabric of each party's position.

Mediators can establish impartiality in any of a number of ways—by helping both parties salvage some part of their respective positions in the face of onslaughts by the opposition; by being equally aggressive in reshaping the parties' respective positions; even by appearing equally villainous to both parties. Impartiality is best maintained by presenting logical arguments for position change that are grounded in experience and practicality. It may be demonstrated by the parties themselves talking about how tough the mediator has been on the positions and arguments of both teams.

That impartiality be preserved is essential. It may be tenuous and endangered, but the mediator and the mediation can go on only as long as acceptability continues. If either party loses confidence in the mediator and no longer believes him to be impartial, the mediator has lost his effectiveness in that case.

Summary

The foregoing catalogue of qualifications may be intimidating to those seeking to enter the field. It is perhaps an idealized version of what the parties hope for in their mediators.

The parties don't always have the experience or sophistication to make the most of the mediators' skills, or even to know when they have qualified mediators. This is particularly true of public sector participants, who tend to be less experienced in collective bargaining.

But if mediation is to continue to merit the support and endorsement of the parties, they must insist upon high standards for mediators. Only through such critical expectations can the true craftsmen be nurtured and encouraged until one day there will no longer be any question of whether mediation is an art or a trade.

4

MOVING TO MEDIATION

As we have emphasized, the goal of negotiations is the resolution by the parties themselves of the dispute that separates them. In order to show how mediators become involved in what everyone declares to be the parties' dispute, we shall examine the ways in which direct negotiations may break down, the methods for selecting the mediator, and the procedures for making contact with the mediator and arranging for the initial mediation session.

Cessation of Direct Negotiations

The cessation of direct negotiations, which is the signal for resort to mediation, may come about in several ways, each of which will help determine how the mediator will enter the scene and what he will do when the mediation process begins. Direct negotiations may end because a previously agreed-upon deadline, or an externally imposed political, statutory, or budget deadline, has been reached. They may end because of a legitimate impasse over how to bridge the gap remaining between the parties. Or they may end because the relationship between the negotiators has so deteriorated and become so hostile that there no longer is any communication between them. Let us look at each of these situations in turn.

Agreed-Upon Deadline

In the private sector there is no magic contract expiration date. That is a function of the parties' agreement and their negotiation of a mutually acceptable duration clause. In some industries coordinated bargaining produces a single deadline for some or all companies. Sometimes the companies and unions in an industry deliberately stagger their contract expiration dates. More often still the expiration date is arrived at by adding the negotiated duration period, say one, two, or three years, to the date on which the agreement is signed—or perhaps to its effective date if its terms are to take effect either before or after date of settlement and contract signing.

If parties in the private sector are unable to reach agreement on a new contract prior to the expiration date of their current agreement, Section 8(d)(3) of Title I of the Labor Management Relations Act comes into play. It requires that the FMCS and any appropriate state mediation agency be notified 30 days prior to contract expiration of any instance where a breakdown in negotiations might result in a strike or lockout. The FMCS is empowered by Section 203(b) of Title II of that Act to "proffer its services. . .either upon its own motion or upon request of one or more of the parties to a dispute." Although it is used in only about 10 percent of all collective bargaining disputes, mediation is a valuable standby tool for maintaining industrial peace.

In the public sector there is usually no such automatic triggering of the mediation step. In fact, because strikes are generally illegal and essential services must be maintained, the contract deadline is far less meaningful in the public sector than in the private sector. The slogan "no contract, no work" is not often heard in the public sector; rather, negotiations are likely to continue in a meandering and desultory fashion with no focus on a meaningful completion date. Thus, the result is the opposite of what occurs with contract deadlines in the private sector.

Reflecting a desire to avoid this inconclusive situation, a number of public sector agreements require that mediation be undertaken on a fixed schedule prior to the contract expiration date. In addition, some state public sector agencies offer mediation services as a matter of course prior to contract deadline, as is done by the FMCS in the private sector.

That the date specified in the contract for commencing mediation has been reached does not necessarily mean that the parties are deadlocked in their negotiations. As is true in the private sector, the automatic triggering of mediation may be premature. The parties may in fact still be engaged in meaningful direct negotiations, jointly anticipating settlement with no expectation of reaching impasse or running beyond the contract expiration date. In such a situation mandatory intervention by a mediator may be detrimental to the negotiating process, forestalling further voluntary exchanges, further compromise, and perhaps even final agreement by solidifying the parties' positions.

Even if called upon to intervene at such a time, most mediators when they become aware of the facts would play a passive role. They would try to ascertain whether there was a reasonable chance of further progress by means of direct negotiations and, if persuaded that there was, probably would merely advise the parties of their continuing availability and willingness to enter the dispute if needed.

Political or Budgetary Deadlines

Public sector employers, unlike those in the private sector, usually have no economic autonomy. They must deal with external authorities to secure financing of the terms and conditions they have agreed upon. The fixed calendar deadlines for submitting budgets, having budgets approved, or having legislatures approve the funding of agreements often influence the timing of negotiations. The parties must allow time for mediation to enhance their prospects for settlement before statutory or legal deadlines are reached. In the New England states, for instance, town meetings held in the spring serve as the legislative and funding bodies of the communities. These meetings create very real settlement deadlines because of the prospect that the town may unilaterally set funding below the level the parties had been contemplating. The parties sometimes schedule their negotiation period to leave time for mediation, if necessary, and perhaps for fact finding as well, to increase the chances of reaching agreement in advance of the town meeting.

In other jurisdictions, where the state legislature may meet for only a portion of the year, or where there is a legislatively mandated deadline for a local or state budget submission, similar time arrangements may be made to increase the prospects of timely agreement.

Usually, however, the parties are sufficiently alert to such deadlines and the need for a mediator's intervention that they need not create contractual deadlines.

Impasses on the Issues

The third occasion for resort to mediation is when the parties reach a legitimate impasse on substantive issues. These impasses, free of rancor between the parties, are the most susceptible to innovative mediation. Such impasses may occur at any time in the parties' negotiations, without regard to contractual, statutory, or budget deadlines. They can occur despite complete good faith on both sides. It may simply be that, despite their best efforts, both sides are adamant.

An impasse is the point where the parties are unable to move from their positions on the outstanding issues or to get movement from the other side. One or both teams presumably recognize that they are stymied and that a third party is needed to suggest alternative positions to induce movement from the intransigent positions both parties have taken, or to help persuade one or both parties of the futility, dangers, or risks of their present postures.

These are the impasses that mediators enjoy the most, and find the most challenging. The parties are still communicating with each other and with the mediator. With such rapport the mediator should be able to secure a detached assessment from each side as to where his efforts should be directed. The mediation process can be most effective when the parties and the mediator are able to work together to get the negotiations off dead center.

Parties' Inability to Communicate

Probably the most frustrating cause of negotiation breakdown, for the parties and the mediator alike, is the parties' loss of the ability to communicate with each other. Such a breakdown does not necessarily coincide with an impasse over the substantive matters being negotiated. It is more likely to occur in advance of a breakdown over substantive issues, when the level of frustration in the relationship is so great that the parties are no longer able even to discuss the merits of their respective positions. If there is long-standing animosity between the two sides, the breakdown may come early in the negotiations, perhaps even before any of the traditional give-and-take. If it is caused by obstinacy or belligerence during the negotiations, it may occur after some or even most issues have been resolved. It may occur because of an ill-timed outburst by a representative of one party against the other. It may come about as a result of a premature strike vote or picketing or a government official's public pledge to freeze wages. In the tensions of some negotiations an action or a remark that would otherwise go unheeded may be enough to produce an impasse.

Selecting the Mediator

Once it is decided to go to mediation, the next step is to determine who the mediator will be. Different procedures may be used.

Private Sector Agencies

In the private sector, the Federal Mediation and Conciliation Service handles most mediation appointments. It assigns staff members, located at various FMCS offices around the nation, who work as full-time mediators. These mediators keep track of negotiations in progress, even before they become inflamed. They become involved in negotiation impasses in a rather routine manner that provides a smooth transition from direct negotiations to mediation. A similar approach is followed by several of the state mediation agencies for private sector disputes with which they are concerned.

Public Sector Agencies

In the public sector, mediators are obtained in different ways. The parties may contact the state agency responsible for mediation when there is one in the jurisdiction; contact the mediator directly; or contact a private designating agency such as the American Arbitration Association, which keeps a roster of available mediators to help the parties in their selection process.

When a state agency is available, one or both parties may request that it designate a mediator. In some jurisdictions the agency has professional full-time mediators on tap to handle disputes. As noted earlier, the seasonal pressures of public sector contract negotiations timed to precede budget, legislative, or school-opening deadlines make it risky to rely exclusively on state agency staff mediators, particularly when the state agency mediators are also assigned to private sector disputes. During peak periods, when the supply of staff mediators is insufficient, many state agencies designate ad hoc nonstaff mediators to close the gap. Under some state statutes these outside mediators are provided without cost to the disputing parties, with the designating agency paying them for their services. Under other state statutes the costs are shared between the state and the parties. Still other statutes provide for payment by the parties themselves; typically they split the mediator's fees and expenses.

When nonstaff mediators are used by the state, it is not unusual for the agency to give the parties some choice in the designation of the mediator. Some agencies provide a list of available mediators and permit the parties to strike names from the list until only a single name remains. That mediator is then designated by the agency. Other agencies invite suggestions from the parties and designate one of the mediators proposed by both sides. State agencies usually will honor a joint request for a particular ad hoc mediator if that person is available.

A number of cities in the United States have neutral agencies similar to the state agencies. These municipal agencies, such as the Office of Collective Bargaining in New York City, provide experienced staff and ad hoc mediators in a manner similar to that of the state agencies.

Selection by the Parties

In states where there is no agency to designate the mediator, the parties must make their own arrangements. Parties unable to agree on contract terms, and perhaps even having communication problems, must nevertheless get together to select a mutually acceptable mediator.

What should the parties look for in selecting a mediator? The qualities that make for a competent mediator have been set forth in

Chapter 3. Which will be given greater weight in making the selection depends to some extent upon the particular preferences and prejudices of the parties.

Some may think they can beat the system by selecting a mediator likely to be inclined toward their position on the disputed issues. They should keep in mind, however, that their perception is probably matched by the other side's perception that the same mediator is unfavorable. They should further recognize that the mediator who sets down a position in the role of fact finder or arbitrator will not be serving as a salesman for that viewpoint when working as a mediator. For example, as an arbitrator I believe strongly in final and binding grievance arbitration, and have recommended final and binding arbitration in some fact-finding reports. But in other circumstances when serving as fact finder, I have recommended adhering to an existing practice of advisory arbitration because of the specific nature of the case and the employer's track record of carrying out every adverse advisory award. And finally, I have served as a mediator where the parties agreed to advisory arbitration or even no arbitration at all. The point is that the mediator's duty is to bring the parties together, and personal beliefs legitimately expressed in another role should not impede the parties' reaching the agreement they prefer.

Recognizing this, the parties probably are better serving themselves and the process by searching for a mediator who will be acceptable to both sides on the basis of reputation for impartiality and possession of the qualities listed in Chapter 3. Persons new to labor negotiations can readily learn about the qualifications of particular mediators by asking other management or labor attorneys or labor relations consultants for their appraisals.

Usually the selection process focuses on ad hoc mediators with established track records for acceptability. But there is likely to be a problem of securing immediate access to the mediator of first choice. The number of such mediators is relatively small, and other disputing parties with similar calendar deadlines may already have booked the most sought-after ad hoc mediators. Availability may also be limited by the mediators' outside commitments, such as teaching or arbitration duties. And there is an additional factor affecting the choice of mediator: The heavy short-term demand for mediators in a number of communities and states at the same time forces the limited number of mediators, whether agency staff or ad hoc, to divide their time among a number of different relationships, devoting perhaps less time to each dispute than they would in the absence of competing demands for their time. In view of such circumstances, the parties may opt for more readily available, but perhaps less experienced, neutrals; or they may seek an extension of the deadline facing them to permit the use of a preferred mediator. While awaiting the mediator of choice, the parties are likely to continue to meet and negotiate directly.

Reserving Mediation Dates

Some parties are farsighted enough to avoid this problem by agreeing on their selection of a mediator before their negotiations reach deadlock. Doing this resolves two problems. First, it permits the parties to work out their selection problem while they are still communicating well and before hostility over substantive issues can spread to the question of mediator selection. Second, it permits early contact with the mediator of choice and thus a better selection of available dates. From the mediator's viewpoint it encourages rational calendar scheduling to permit adequate time for the dispute, and an opportunity to control travel and work load.

Under this arrangement the parties ask the mediator to hold the agreed-upon dates in reserve for their case. In cases where I have been asked to do this, I offer the parties two choices. Either I will hold the dates until another set of clients asks for them, at which time the reserving clients must confirm their reservation or lose it. Or I will make a firm commitment, placing the responsibility upon the reservers to withdraw their reservation by an agreed-upon date or risk paying a cancellation fee for tardy surrender of the dates and my resulting loss of work opportunity.

Such a reservation system assures the parties of the mediator of their choice in the event their negotiations reach an impasse. If they then resolve the dispute by themselves, they simply call the mediator and advise that they no longer need the reserved dates. Parties opting to take this course with a mediator who charges a cancellation fee should be prepared to pay it if required to do so. The usual fee is compensation for one half to a full day at the mediator's daily rate for the day or days reserved if cancellation is received too late for the mediator to schedule other work for the days in question. The cancellation deadline may vary from 48 hours to as much as a month in advance of the reserved dates.

Another procedure that helps to secure a preferred mediator when needed is for the teams to agree on a number of dates when they are available for mediation. Once they have agreed on such dates, they can develop a list of mediators who are acceptable to both teams and then contact them one by one in some agreed-upon order until they find the first one that is available on the specified dates. In this way it is often possible to secure very early mediation dates from mediators who otherwise might be unavailable unless other parties cancelled at the last minute. This procedure has the advantage of securing a preferred mediator on short notice without risking the expense and annoyance of a cancellation charge.

Mediator Selection Through the AAA

If the relationship between the parties prevents their agreeing on a mediator, it may become necessary to use the facilities of a neutral organization to secure one. The leading choice for this process is the American Arbitration Association (AAA), which will provide a list of qualified mediators tailored to meet any specifications set forth by the parties, such as residence in a specific geographical area or experience in, for example, municipal finance, education, or firefighting problems.

Under the AAA selection process, an identical list of 12 names is provided to both parties. Each side then lists its numerical preference of the names on the list and returns it to the AAA. The Association then designates the parties' highest mutual choice as the mediator for their dispute. For its services the AAA charges a modest fee, which is typically split by the parties.

Initial Contact With the Mediator

Once the mediator has been selected or designated, the next step is establishing contact. In the case of designation by a state or municipal agency or by the AAA, neither party need contact the mediator about availability or to advise him of the selection. The designating agency handles these details, and may serve as a go-between in arranging with the parties for the dates of the mediation as well as the hour and place of the first meeting.

In jurisdictions where the parties select the mediator directly, they must also make the arrangements as to date, time, and place of meeting with the mediator. Parties familiar with the process and comfortable with each other and with the mediator may have little difficulty in handling this initial contact. One spokesperson will simply say to the other, "If you have time today, would you contact her?" or, "I'll give him a call this afternoon and see if he wants to do it, and when."

But in relationships that are not so compatible, or where the parties are new to the process, or where they do not know the mediator, the initial contact can be a matter of concern or suspicion. One party may be suspicious that the other party will get "first crack" at the mediator and provide a prejudiced assessment of their dispute. For the mediator it is not unusual to receive a one-sided view of the parties' dispute, such as, "The only thing holding us up is their position on insurance, but we understand that once you come into the picture it will provide the face saver they need for dropping their position and accepting ours."

Mediators are skeptical of such assertions, and so fears that one side will get a leg up by speaking to the mediator out of the presence of the other side are generally groundless. As a matter of fact, it makes little difference to the mediator or the mediation process whether the mediator is approached by one or both parties in the initial contact. The parties, however, may need reassurance that the mediator has not been unduly influenced by a one-sided communication. If so, more formal procedures for making the initial contact are useful. Thus, the parties may send a joint letter or make a conference call to the mediator. Arrangements for the spokespersons to meet together with the mediator can also be made by a secretary or someone not involved in the merits of the dispute.

What is covered during the initial discussion with the mediator either jointly or separately, by phone or in person, varies with the situation. At the minimum, arrangements are made for the place and time to start the mediation.

Arranging the Place

The mediator ordinarily will have little concern for the location of the session, provided it is acceptable to the parties and there is enough space. There needs to be a room for each side and one for the mediator's caucuses with the spokespersons. The parties may be reluctant to use facilities belonging to one of them, not so much because it is enemy turf but because annoying interruptions are likely. When there is a prospect of all-night sessions, it makes sense for the parties to make arrangements at a local hotel having food and sleeping facilities.

Experienced parties usually follow an established format of their own in selecting and agreeing on the location and merely tell the mediator where the session will be. Inexperienced parties may haggle over this question or turn to the mediator to make the arrangements, or at least set the specifications for the facilities.

Arranging the Time

The time for starting the mediation may also create problems. Often the employer will not want to meet during the workday, particularly if it expects the presence of an elected body such as a school board or city council whose members work at other jobs. The union, on the other hand, may insist on its team being released from work to attend a daytime session and be unwilling to meet at night on personal time. Night sessions are particularly irksome to employees if they are expected to work the next day. The fact that the sessions may well run long into the night may impress the parties with the importance of bringing the teams together for as many hours as is possible. In the end the disputants will probably agree to a starting time as early as is convenient to the mediator. Since mediators usually charge for each day made available to the parties, it makes financial sense to start when the workday begins. Ordinarily that means a morning start if the mediator has cleared the full day for the parties.

The length of the daily sessions may also be a problem requiring clarification and an understanding. Although the parties may agree to mediation for fixed time periods or under certain clock deadlines, it generally is preferable if the closing time of each session is flexible. A party may be unwilling to work through the night—although the parties tend initially to look upon all-night sessions with greater equanimity than do mediators—yet a prolonged session may make sense when the parties are close to agreement. Even for the mediator all-night sessions have some appeal; the parties tend to get tired, and under the pressure of exhaustion to become more reasonable.

Duration of the Mediation

Duration of the mediation process is another issue for preliminary discussion. In the private sector the duration of the mediation is usually determined by the contract expiration date and the strike deadline it creates; the longer the mediation, the greater the likelihood of a strike. The tendency in the public sector, because of the absence of a strike deadline, is to drag out the mediation. Each side is encouraged to keep trying for a little bit more. The absence of realistic final deadlines is one of the greatest handicaps to effective and efficient mediation in the public sector. To compensate for this, mediators and the parties frequently seek to create deadlines. One way is to use out-of-town mediators, whose available time is limited by flight schedules and whose departure ends the mediation. In one mediation case I announced a departure on a certain flight, was not believed, did leave, and a strike ensued. While I regretted the consequence of my announced departure, since that time I have never had any questions raised over my personal deadlines for ending mediation, either by those parties or by others who heard of the incident. The luxury of out-of-town mediators may not be available to parties using a government-provided mediator; but it is to obtain one that some parties opt for private mediators. The ever-ticking meter of the self-employed mediator may also provide a needed stimulus to settlement.

Another device the parties may discuss when scheduling the mediation is a limit on the number of days to be set aside for the mediation, which frees the representatives and the mediator to schedule other activities for the time thereafter. Moreover, as the last of the allotted days draws nearer, the pressure to settle increases. This is particularly true if the only dates available thereafter are months away, or on such undesirable dates as the Friday after Thanksgiving or the day before Christmas.

Although the scheduling of a number of mediation dates at the outset may mean that there will be little movement on the earlier dates, the alternative of repeatedly scheduling one additional date is even less attractive, leading the parties to believe that an extra day will always be made available and foreclosing any real sense of finality.

Cost of Mediation

The cost of the mediation may also be a matter for initial discussion with the parties. This is not a problem in jurisdictions where the state provides the mediator without charge to the parties. Where the mediator is hired on a fee-for-service basis, as are most ad hoc mediators, it is a concern. Mediators charge fixed fees, usually on a daily basis. In most cases the mediator who also works as an arbitrator charges the same fee for mediating as for arbitrating; but some arbitrators have higher daily rates for mediation work because of the greater pressure and intensity of the work, and also because a day spent in arbitration usually is accompanied by a "study day"—i.e., time needed to prepare the award—which is lost when mediating.

Inasmuch as most neutrals charge by the day rather than by the hour, the question arises as to how many hours there are in a mediator's day. Some mediators charge for an eight-hour day, while others charge for a six-hour day. Thus a mediation which runs around the clock may be charged to the parties as the equivalent of either three or four workdays. It is advisable to secure in advance from the mediators the basis of their rate structure and charges. The mediator, of course, must be reimbursed for all travel expenses incurred for a case, and occasionally a fee is charged for travel time as well.

Summary

Once the parties have come to the point when direct negotiations have ended, they face the task of mediator selection. They are relieved of this responsibility in the private sector and in public sector jurisdictions where staff mediators are designated by the FMCS or state agencies. But in states and jurisdictions where there is no agency, the disputing parties must either agree on a mediator or turn to a neutral organization such as the American Arbitration Association to assist them in selection.

Once a mediator has been designated, the parties, together with the mediator, must work out the details of time, place, and costs of the mediation. The way these details are handled may be significant in either facilitating or exacerbating the parties' efforts to bring an end to their dispute.

5

PREPARING FOR MEDIATION

When the parties have agreed with the mediator on the time and place for the initiation of the mediation, they must prepare for the sessions. It is important that some of the preparation be joint, even if it was a breakdown in communication between the parties that caused the impasse. The parties must determine which issues they have already settled and the status of the settlement agreements, and they must determine which issues are unresolved. They must also agree upon any ground rules for the mediation that they wish the mediator to follow. They may even find it necessary to turn to the mediator prior to the initial mediation session to help them resolve any disputes they may have on how to proceed in the mediation itself.

Tentative Agreements

If the parties have had any success during their direct negotiations, it is likely that they have reached agreement on some or even most of the items that had originally been in dispute. These agreements might have been to withdraw a proposal, to adopt a proposal in its entirety, or to insert into the contract a compromise somewhere between the original positions. Agreements to drop proposals or to insert new terms into the agreement are called "tentative agreements" when reached in the course of negotiations but prior to final agreement. They are tentative because they do not stand on their own and are meaningless and unenforceable until they are incorporated into the final agreement covering the full range of agreement on wages, hours, and working conditions.

Use of the term "tentative agreement" has another important implication— namely, that the issue in question is not irrevocably settled until agreement has been reached on all other provisions of the contract. So many clauses of a collective bargaining agreement are interdependent that it would be virtually impossible to keep discussing every element of the disputed positions until there was full agreement on the entire package.

Let us take an example: the union and the employer are discussing wage rates for the forthcoming contract term. In the course of their negotiations they agree that the prevailing increase in the surrounding communities, 6 percent, should apply to their settlement as well. They then initial that understanding as a "tentative agreement." But then they begin to discuss the health insurance package and a union demand for dental insurance, a benefit none of the surrounding communities has granted to its employees. The employer objects to this demand because of its cost, 1 percent of payroll, which it claims will place it out of line with the surrounding communities. The union is so anxious to have the dental insurance that it offers to reduce the already agreed-upon wage increase from 6 percent to 5 percent in exchange for dental insurance, and the employer agrees. Had the agreement on the 6-percent wage increase been firm and final, the employer could not have offered to provide the additional cost of dental insurance as part of the 6 percent. Thus, a "tentative agreement" is tabled as if it were final, but it may be reopened if a subsequently discussed provision has an impact upon it.

The contribution of the tentative-agreement concept toward facilitating the mediation process is substantial. Frequently one of the parties entering mediation will insist that, since direct negotiations have failed, all tentative agreements are null and void, and that all the initial proposals are back on the table. If both parties take this position it will be as if there had never been tentative understandings. It is more likely, however, that only one party will favor wiping the slate clean, with the other party willing to adhere to the tentative agreements. This is one of the issues that the parties should endeavor to resolve prior to the mediation in their exchanges on ground rules. Otherwise, mediating the status of the earlier understandings may become one of the mediator's first tasks.

Mediators generally do not like to reactivate issues that the parties themselves have put to rest, if only tentatively. Not only does it mean more work for the mediator to have them back on the table as additional items to be mediated, more important, it often means creating more conflict. Most mediators would therefore seek to secure agreement between the parties to let sleeping dogs lie.

Reasons for Not Reopening

The arguments mediators would use to persuade the party seeking to reopen tentatively settled issues are the following:

1. To put them back on the table will reopen closed wounds. It will rekindle hostility that has died down, and this might have an adverse impact on the issues still open.

2. It will prolong the mediation, thereby delaying final agreement. If there is a time deadline in the negotiations, the reopening of issues might prevent a timely settlement on the open issues. In addition, it will increase the cost of the mediation by forcing the mediator to devote time to reopened issues.

3. Probably the best argument for preserving the previously negotiated tentative agreements during mediation is that these agreements were the parties own, reached in direct negotiations and presumably acceptable, even if only marginally. To reopen these items sacrifices a mutually tolerable result and risks a different outcome which, in the light of the passage of time and the emphasis on different issues, may be less satisfactory. The spirit of accommodation which led to the tentative agreements in the earlier days of direct negotiations may have been eroded. There is now sufficient conflict between the parties to justify the intervention of a mediator. Now, with the parties having their eyes on the troublesome outstanding issues it may be more difficult to secure agreement on issues that seemed less controversial earlier.

4. The earlier agreements are only tentative. If the subsequent negotiations cast one of the tentative agreements in a different light, it may still be reopened for modification. Final agreement is contingent on settlement of all issues.

Mediators are usually successful in preserving existing tentative agreements by using some or all of the foregoing arguments. But if there is resistance, they can achieve the same goal by declining to deal with them at the start of mediation. The mediator can say: "I would rather not get into those issues now. Let's table them for the time being and get to (whatever is outstanding)." Usually the mention of an outstanding issue will cause the parties to switch gears and turn their attention to more volatile subjects, bypassing the issue of tentative agreements for the time being.

The parties are usually eager to resolve the more pressing outstanding issues. The mediator's assurance that there will be time to get back to the subjects of the tentative agreements is usually sufficient to permit the parties to go forward with the open issues. And when all the other issues are disposed of, and the parties are finally confronted with the prospect of reopening already-closed matters, they are likely to accede to a suggestion that everything be kept as agreed to and that settlement of the entire contract be assumed.

Even if this ploy does not work, it is unlikely that all the tentative agreements will be reopened. It may well be possible to limit the number of reopeners, as in one case where the parties agreed that each side could reopen two tentatively settled items. The parties are usually satisfied with the opportunity to have another crack at one or two items that were particularly irksome when earlier agreed to. On the other hand, since the same opportunity is afforded to the other side, the prospect of giving the other side a second bite at the apple may be enough to avoid reopening altogether.

Identifying the Open Issues

Once the parties have determined how to treat the items that had been tentatively agreed upon during direct negotiations, they must ascertain the status of the remaining proposals—those that will be the subjects of the mediation.

Joint Review of the Issues

Joint review of the remaining issues is helpful for a number of reasons. First, it forces the teams into what is in fact another negotiating session even though direct negotiations have ostensibly come to an end. During the cataloging of where each stands on the remaining issues, the two sides may find that they are not as far apart as they had thought, that a position can be modified and that there may be certain tradeoffs. In short, they may find themselves back in negotiations. Such an exchange may be particularly useful if conducted by the team leaders, without the aid, or impediment, of their teams.

Second, the joint review may reveal that some of the items ostensibly in dispute were in fact the subject of tentative agreements; agreements may have been reached but not initialed by the spokespersons. More likely, however, the review will disclose proposals that were included on the teams' "wish lists"—that is, items desired by the constituents of one team or the other but not expected to be in the final contract. After being proposed and argued for, such items may have been omitted from later package proposals but never formally withdrawn. The issue review session provides a convenient forum for adding items no longer in contention to the list of tentative agreements.

Third, the review provides an opportunity to determine which items on the disputed list are not proper items for insertion in the contract. These may involve matters of employer policies, or issues controlled by statute or government regulation. Some items may in effect be pending grievance matters, items that should have been handled by the submission of grievances or that are so unusual or personalized that they are unlikely to occur again. It makes sense for the parties to agree to remove those items from the list of issues for mediation, and to seek alternative procedures for their resolution. Some can best be referred to a joint study committee, some disposed of through letters of understanding, and some processed as grievances, perhaps with the employer dropping any challenge to their timeliness.

Fourth, the review provides the mediator with a concise list of the issues in dispute and, in effect, commits the teams to work from that list without adding new or expanded proposals thereafter. It also avoids the wasting of time at the start of the mediation while the spokespersons seek to determine exactly where they were when direct negotiations broke off.

Early examination of the status of the proposals and the identification of those issues that are to be on the table is also calculated to help the parties prepare for mediation. The joint session on issue identification is particularly important when one or both parties have opted to bring in new spokespersons for the mediation. Their involvement and fresh perspective may lead to new movement on issues that had become frozen under their predecessors.

Few or Many Issues to Mediate

There are two schools of thought on the number of issues that should be submitted to mediation. One school takes the position that a party is better served by submitting all remaining issues no matter how large or small to the mediator. The other school favors paring down the issues. Unquestionably, the former course is easier to adhere to politically within the negotiating team. It assures the various constituencies that the team is fighting to the end for their pet issues, thus enhancing the standing of the spokesperson. It also allows the spokesperson to get off the hook for any surrender of a pet issue by making the mediator the "fall guy" in any failure to sell it to the other side. But whether the political benefits to the spokesperson and the team are worth the additional time and cost spent in special handling of potential washout items can be questioned.

It is not merely that the presentation and consideration of a long list of open items is time-consuming; it also hinders the other party's ability to make a reasonable response because that party has no way of ascertaining which of the items are important and which are not. Neither party is helped if a minor item is mistakenly viewed as an item of substance and responded to with the other team's main settlement offer. There is also a question of whether such tenacity on items of questionable merit falsely raises the expectations of their proponents.

The contrary view, that the team should pare down its list of demands to exclude the frivolous and unattainable, requires a measure of discipline and predictability as to what can realistically be achieved. Although it may take the team more time to weed out the fluff, this may result in shorter mediation and in lower costs. It may also send the message to the other team that the items which survived the culling process are all of high priority.

Joint Issues List for the Mediator

Although the above described review of the unresolved issues may help the parties determine what is realistic and what should be abandoned, one more step facilitates the process of focusing on the most critical issues. That is the preparation of a joint document for the mediator setting forth the unresolved issues. It is developed by the spokespersons and should be given to the mediator prior to the commencement of the mediation.

Like a joint meeting to identify the unresolved issues, the joint drafting of an issues document offers an opportunity for the spokespersons to discuss the troublesome issues and possibly resolve some of them. Too often the meetings between the teams are marked by only general discussion of issues without consideration of specific language or of possible alternatives. Requiring the explication of proposals and positions in one document encourages the parties to consider, perhaps for the first time, the specifics of the other side's proposals. The examination of proposed language occasionally elicits a response or submission of counter language which not only furthers the direct negotiations but may stimulate accommodation and even agreement.

The issues document is of direct benefit to the mediator. It permits the creation of an "issues book" that accurately reflects the parties' respective stands just prior to mediation and, if sent out in time, enables the mediator to get up to speed even before actually meeting with the parties. This not only saves time and money but also may lead to the disposition of some of the listed items.

The mediator's issue book is most useful if prepared on an issue-by-issue basis, stating the relevant provision, if any, in the present agreement and the proposals for change offered by either or both parties. The author's preferred format for the issue book is a three-ring notebook, with excerpts from the present agreement taped to the top center of the page and union and management proposals taped on either side thereof. In relationships where I have mediated more than once, the spokespersons send me, in advance of the first mediation session, either the raw material for preparing the issues book or the document itself laid out in the manner described above. This enables me to read through the language of the present agreement and compare it with the proposals for change. Then when we meet I have a good idea of the essentials of each disputed issue. When the parties do not provide an issues book I usually develop one during the first break, using my own scissors and tape. The document serves as a handy place for making notations of what is said in mediating sessions. It is useful for note-taking as well and for writing down what is given to me for transmittal to the other side.

Although an issues book is a valuable tool both for the parties and for the mediator, there are obviously relationships where the hostility between the parties does not permit the joint development of such a document. In those situations the mediator must ferret out the parties' positions on the issues in dispute at the initial sessions. But the time saved by the preparation of an issues book and the possibility that some issues will be resolved by the parties during that preparation suggests that it is in the parties' best interests to put aside their antagonisms to develop an issues list if they can.

Joint Ground Rules

The meeting between the spokespersons on the issues to be submitted to mediation can have other value as well. It provides an opportunity for them to develop any ground rules they wish to utilize during the mediation. In some matters, such as whether the sessions are to be public or private, and contacts with the press, they may decide to continue into the mediation the same ground rules they observed during direct negotiations. In other matters, such as opportunities for press briefings by the mediator, they may set new rules for themselves and the mediator.

Public or Private Sessions

Whether the sessions are to be public or private is a matter that should be addressed before the first mediation session. If this is done, it is possible to avoid the inevitable confrontation between outsiders protesting their right to observe and the parties that are directly in interest.

In the private sector, decades of negotiation and mediation have led to certain expectancies concerning the parties' conduct which are subject to challenge when the process is imported to the public sector. A prime example of this phenomenon is the tolerance of the presence of outside parties. Private sector mediation is recognized as a bilateral relationship with the mediator being the only outsider. This tradition has grown from the parties' joint recognition of the privacy of their relationship and from the disinterest of outsiders as to the terms or conditions of employment they agree to. Certainly it can be argued that the community in which the enterprise operates, as represented by the chamber of commerce, the press, or government agencies, has an interest or a stake in the outcome, or that a rival union supported by a minority of the employees has a right to observe the proceedings. But private sector ground rules have almost invariably excluded them from mediation sessions.

External pressures are stronger in the public sector: the press, taxpayers associations, parents alliances, and other citizen groups tend to seek entry into the mediation, to participate in or at least to observe the parties' deliberations. Taxes, the quality of education, and police and fire protection may be directly affected.

In some jurisdictions the outsiders draw support from leaders of organizations that have participated in the operation of the community, or from enactment of "sunshine laws" that have created an entitlement to participation in governmental workings. Although most sunshine laws explicitly, or by judicial interpretation or by practice, have come to exclude outside pressure groups from negotiations and mediation, there are always groups that insist on a right to participate.

The Mediator's Preference

The mediator's role in such controversies does not empower him to make decisions to admit or exclude outsiders. If both parties agree to let outsiders participate or be present, which is unlikely, the mediator, recognizing that the process belongs to the parties, will probably refrain from expressing a contrary view. Similarly, if both parties agree to the exclusion of outside groups, the mediator, probably with greater conviction, will do what he can to keep the outsiders out. Certainly if the parties agree in advance upon closed sessions and an outside party appears at the first session asserting a right under law to participate, it is not the mediator's place to enforce that right. That party should go to court to secure a stay of the closed mediation if the law so requires.

If one of the parties wants the participation of outside groups and the other side objects, they may have to refer the issue to the mediator at or perhaps prior to the initial session. If the authority to decide the question of outside participation is granted to the mediator, the parties have invested him with an arbitrator's authority for that issue only. If they have not so authorized him, the resolution of the issue becomes his introductory mediatory effort. If it is deferred to the first session, it may be a mediating effort that involves not only the parties but the outside groups as well.

The mediator's task will be much simplified—as will be that of the parties—if the proceedings are closed. The outside party or parties have no responsibility for the implementation of provisions governing wages, hours, and working conditions; they have no accountability in terms of the enforcement of the bilateral agreement; they have little or no understanding of the give and take of the process; and they usually have little more than an advisory or policy-articulating role to play. More important, it is inconsistent with the process to permit them to attend mediation sessions, let alone caucuses with the mediator. To the extent that they claim to represent the public, taxpayers, students, or the consumer of the public services at issue, they are redundant. Such representation is the function and the responsibility of the employer, the elected or otherwise designated officials represented by the management team. Thus, to permit outside groups to participate results in double public representation.

To the extent that they claim to represent the consumers of service seeking greater numbers of welfare workers or shorter hours for police or fireman, the outside groups are also redundant, since the unions presumably have the same goals. The mediator probably would urge the team arguing for the presence of the outside groups to modify its position.

Besides exclusion, the parties could agree to other procedures that would permit negotiations to continue on a bilateral basis. One would be to invite a representative of each outside group to join one team or the other as a consultant. Unless the parties have contractual restrictions on the numbers and composition of their respective teams, each side generally has freedom to select the members of its team. Another possibility would be to permit the leaders of the outside groups to make a statement for the record at the opening session and then depart. Yet a third possibility would be to allow the representatives to remain as silent observers of the joint sessions with agreed-upon conditions as to numbers, note taking (or note passing), and role or presence when the teams meet separately with the mediator. Finally, if the mediator is unsuccessful in working out a consensus on this subject, he still holds the final card. All he need do to derail the outsiders' insistence on participation is run the mediation in caucus meetings with the teams separately and, thus, without the outside intervenors. In the most persistent situations the team leaders and the mediator can simply agree to meet elsewhere.

The Media

A related issue which should be resolved prior to the start of mediation is relations with the media. The same problems that arise with outside groups arise with the media. Although they will probably not seek to testify or ask questions during the proceedings, they will want to attend and observe the joint sessions as well as the caucuses.

The problems with the media are perhaps even greater because of the commitment to report events from within the mediation. The desire of the press and other media representatives to report on the proceedings is bound to interfere with the role of the mediator and the structuring and timing of the movement toward settlement more than would the presence of a pressure group. Although the media certainly have an obligation to report the news, and the public has a commensurate right to be informed, the presence of the media in the mediation sessions alters their character. It also hampers the efforts of the mediator to work privately with the parties in order to facilitate their movement toward settlement. For example, if the union proclaimed in a joint session that it would never agree to a management proposal with respect to the contracting out of work, a media report of that vow could freeze that position, which otherwise might be more flexible and negotiable as the price of a final settlement. The problem is made more dramatic when there is public concern on an issue, such as a wage freeze, that a team leader for management with political aspirations might endorse to the press, thereby compounding management's negotiating problems.

If the parties at the outset informed the mediator that they had agreed to permit the media to attend the proceedings, the mediator would probably accept their arrangement. But he would point out that the parties were creating additional problems for themselves, and would reserve the right to have private conversations with one or both spokespersons, or even with the teams, if he deemed it necessary.

The parties' and the mediator's concern about a media presence in the mediation proceeding should not be interpreted as a judgment that the media do not have a legitimate concern about the proceedings. Good relations with the media are important to both parties and can be helpful to the mediation process. There is a public right to know what is going on in negotiations involving taxes and public services which must be balanced against the parties' right to privacy in seeking accommodation on a new contract. A sympathetic media can do much to deter efforts by pressure groups to participate and can be helpful to the participants and the process by reporting how the negotiations are proceeding, by reporting on the final agreement, or even by reporting a breakdown in negotiations. Media representatives who are respected by the parties and the mediator and whose needs are accommodated will be far less likely to try an "end run" around the spokespersons to find out from team members what is going on and then report such one-sided perceptions as fact. Irresponsible reporting can destroy the privacy of mediation and turn the process into a barrage of press and TV attacks and headline hunting by the spokespersons.

Briefings by the Mediator

The parties must therefore assure that the role of the media, if not helpful, will at least be neutral and nondestructive. The fairest way of doing this is for the mediator to hold periodic, perhaps daily, meetings with representatives of the media to provide them with the copy, film footage, or press linage they need to fulfill their reportorial function. Not only does that accommodation meet their reportage needs, but it frees them from the need to contact individual team members and provides a forum that can be used by the mediator to encourage or nudge the parties a bit.

The most common arrangement is for the teams to agree that they will suspend their contacts with the media and let the mediator speak for them, presumably in the periodic press, radio, and/or TV briefings. In such briefings the mediator usually will provide a general assessment of how the mediation is proceeding, describing the tenor of the exchanges, the prospects for settlement, and the like. Details and provocative statements generally are avoided, and "penetrating questions" usually are fended off.

Compromise arrangements worked out by the parties might permit media representatives to sit in on the joint opening session to take notes or tape or film the participants' opening remarks. Media representatives also might be permitted to attend sessions occasionally to film background footage for showing on the news without reference to content being discussed; and to do background pieces on the mediator or the team leaders from time to time without reference to the substantive issues.

Handling Leaks

Arrangements with the media generally are made in good faith by the spokespersons, are acceptable to the mediator, and are lived up to by members of both teams. Occasionally, however, a militant partipant on one of the teams, either for personal glory or to advance his side's cause, will breach the press accord and "leak" information to the media. Sometimes a media representative may search for a leak. It is not difficult to find a source of inside information in situations where the union maintains a telephone hot line to inform its members of the status of negotiations. Members of the media have only to secure the hot line number and call in as though they were union members.

Lamentably, there is little the parties or the mediator can do to plug up or punish such leaks even though they may have the effect of destroying the privacy and effectiveness of the mediation. The process is the parties'; and the disciplinary problem is theirs; the mediator who wishes to continue in the case can do little. He could, of course, withdraw, or threaten to do so if there is a recurrence, but such action would certainly have a greater detrimental impact on the negotiation process than any unattributed or denied press, radio, or TV report.

Responsible media representatives, seeking to observe the accord, will either ignore leaks or at least seek confirmation from the mediator before making them public. They want the mediation to be effective, and they use background information constructively. They respect "off the record" confidences, and they are welcome companions for the mediator during the long intervals of team caucuses. In any event, they quickly lose interest in the proceedings, reducing the whole mountainous issue to a mole hill.

Transcribing the Proceedings

Another matter that must be resolved at the initial session, if it was not dealt with by the parties at the outset of their direct negotiations, is that of transcribing the proceedings. The recording of the proceedings by court stenographer or by tape recorder, like the presence of the media, encourages the spokespersons to make long, self-serving pronouncements and declarations that impede the effort to reach a settlement. As experienced parties recognize, such verbatim reporting serves little purpose when most of the action occurs in private conversations and hallway caucuses. In fact, the presence of a stenographer or the operation of a tape recorder during joint sessions or one-party meetings tends to increase the frequency of sessions beyond the range of the reporter or recorder. In addition, experienced parties recognize that agreement is possible in some situations only if the language is vague, the parties being unwilling or unable to agree on the meaning of the words. Their clear intent is to defer to the future the interpretation of the agreement. A transcript of the proceedings would undermine that intent, invite long-winded speeches, miss crucial off-the-record discussions, and perhaps even constitute an impediment to settlement. For these reasons, there are some mediators who would insist on the right to conduct off-the-record conversations and caucuses, beyond the reach of the stenographer, even where the parties have agreed to have a verbatim transcript.

The same rationale applies to tape recordings made by one of the teams. Such one-sided recordings place the other party at a distinct disadvantage both in the mediation and in later discussions, when what was said in negotiations might be crucial to a resolution of a grievance over the meaning of certain contract language.

Most mediators, if requested to decide whether transcriptions or recordings are to be made, will decide against them. And although few would refuse to mediate solely because recordings were made of joint team meetings, most mediators would not permit recordings of the entire proceedings, including private caucuses or conversations. Off-the-record exchanges are too important an element in conflict resolution to be sacrificed merely to satisfy a party's desire for a verbatim record.

Summary

The process of agreeing on the status of the issues in dispute—those resolved and those pending—provides a valuable opportunity for a private session between the spokespersons prior to the mediation. That session may prove effective in bringing about further agreement on some, or perhaps even all, of the outstanding issues.

It also provides a valuable opportunity for the spokespersons to clarify the ground rules to govern the forthcoming mediation. In most cases the ground rules in effect during direct negotiations can be carried forward without change. But in some matters the parties may seek to change the rules, or introduce new rules tailored to the mediation.

Agreements on these matters reached by the parties will probably prove acceptable to the mediator. If there are conflicts over the ground rules, resolving these conflicts may be the initial test of the mediator's skills at the first session.

Even if the spokespersons are unable to reach agreement on all the ground rules to govern the forthcoming mediation, their efforts to do so may lead to an enhanced sense of mutual confidence and, possibly, further direct discussions prior to the first date set for mediation. Whether or not this is the case, the good will engendered in this initial session should prove a valuable asset for each of the spokespersons at a later stage in the proceedings.

6

THE FIRST MEDIATION SESSION

Even though mediation may be a routine way of life for the mediator, it is likely to be a new experience for most or all of the individuals on the respective teams. The spokespersons' prior exposure to mediation may depend on whether they are professional advocates or whether they have moved up through the teams' hierarchies. Team members may have heard about prior mediations or spoken to people who have been through the process, but they are probably inexperienced and perhaps nervous about what is to take place and their role in it.

It is therefore important that the team members be set at ease and made to feel comfortable with their role in the process. The initial mediation session provides an opportunity for the mediator to explain the process and to build the personal confidence and rapport that will be so important as the process continues.

In those jurisdictions where the initial arrangements for the mediation have been made through a neutral agency, and in those cases where there have been no preliminary discussions as described in Chapters 4 and 5 because of the parties' unavailability, or because of their hostility, the first mediation session may also constitute the first meeting of the spokespersons and the mediator.

Preliminary Meeting

Most mediators prefer to meet jointly with the spokespersons but without the teams prior to the start of the formal mediation. This session may be held on an earlier date or on the same day as the first scheduled mediation session. Mediators often propose that such a session be held at a restaurant over dinner or even breakfast to provide a more informal, relaxed atmosphere.

The purpose of the session is to develop rapport with the spokespersons and to resolve any procedural problems before the start of the formal mediation. This is the time for the spokespersons to advise the mediator of any ground rules the teams have agreed upon for the mediation, and to seek the mediator's help in resolving any disputes over ground rules prior to the start of the first session. The session also provides an opportunity for the parties and the mediator to work out the schedule of sessions.

Settlement Exploration

The most important purpose of the session is to provide an off-the-record opportunity for the three to commence discussion on the substantive elements of the dispute. There may have been phone calls between the mediator and the individual spokespersons to arrange the mediation dates, and perhaps to give a general indication of the types of issues in dispute, but in most cases this session will be the first face-to-face meeting between the three.

If there is obvious rigidity in the spokespersons' positions or hostility in their relationship at this stage, the mediator may merely ask for a brief summary of the issues in dispute. If, on the other hand, there appears to be some flexibility and willingness to make concessions on the part of the team leaders, the mediator may actually begin his mediation effort. The spokespersons on their own or at the mediator's urging may give a thumbnail sketch of the items in dispute or go into detail about their respective positions; they may list their priorities among the remaining issues; or they may be silent on substantive matters. The mediator will welcome any insights that the spokespersons are willing to share, as long as each is present to respond to the other's statements. If there is a long-standing relationship between the mediator and the spokespersons, discussions as to what it will take to resolve the dispute can be more frank. The mediator may suggest or request a grouping of the issues or an indication of the parties' priorities, and may encourage the spokespersons to have further negotiations. There may be an inquiry about the role of external power sources, such as the management board, and a request that they be present during the mediation or easily accessible if necessary.

Spokespersons' Response

Much depends in such discussions on the role of the spokespersons. If they are active participants in the parties' continuing relationship, they may be too embroiled in that relationship to provide the objective assessment of the situation that the mediator needs. But if they are removed from the day-to-day operation of the enterprise—if, for example, they are attorneys representing the parties in negotiations—it may be possible to get some movement at the preliminary session. If both spokespersons are new outsiders, the mediator can capitalize on their personal hopes for a settlement and avoidance of a strike or other escalation of the conflict. In such relationships the spokespersons usually are eager to resolve the dispute and get on with their other work. Clearly they have their orders and their limitations, but they also have independent views as to how far both parties are willing to go. If the mediator can extract an honest appraisal of the prospects from both spokespersons, it may be helpful in moving toward the settlement. If not the best forum for undertaking such explorations, the preliminary session does provide an opportunity for the mediator to induce the spokespersons to talk more freely than they might in a mediation session with their respective teams present.

The mediator in such settlement explorations usually accepts the spokespersons as the legitimate representatives of their respective clients' interests. It would be inappropriate and distrustful to question their representative capacity or to go to their principals to monitor or verify the legitimacy of their credentials. In a process so strongly based on trust, the mediator is duty bound to accept the spokespersons' representations of authority and negotiate with them in the manner that is best suited to achieving the joint goal of settlement. Although such off-the-record discussions might seem to undercut the negotiation process, in reality they are the essence of negotiation with the representatives of the negotiating teams.

Sessions in which the author was a participant have run the gamut from a very brief meeting during which the spokespersons refused to talk about any of the disputed items, to a meeting marked by an outpouring of offers of compromise that were pursued to a settlement in the preliminary session. In the latter case the preliminary meeting lasted several hours, with the spokespersons running to consult with their respective teams every hour or so and to assure them that we were just working out procedural details and would start the mediation session shortly.

It is not unusual for spokespersons who are professional negotiators to explain to the mediator individually or even jointly that they themselves could resolve the disputed issues, without difficulty, but that their respective teams were unwilling to make the necessary compromises. In such cases they may seek to enlist the mediator in structuring a scenario that will permit them to bring their respective teams to the positions the spokespersons recognize will achieve settlement. Some mediators flatly refuse to partake in such arrangements. Most, however, understand that their function is not to arbitrate or impose a third party's resolution, and are willing to help the two designated representatives reach what they consider to be an appropriate settlement. It is not the mediator's place to impede a settlement the team representatives wish to achieve. The mediator in such an excercise may be asked to call for a caucus at a particular juncture, or to propose consideration of the issues in a certain order, or to avoid a certain issue until a later point. In the author's experience, spokespersons who plot a complete scenario right through to settlement may be too far ahead of their teams. The route frequently becomes blocked by unforeseen problems, and the scenario has to be abandoned or recast from time to time.

Yet the mediator's responsibility is to the parties through the representatives whom they have designated. The prudent course for the mediator is usually to accept the spokespersons' greater familiarity with the teams and the issues and, if persuaded of their good-faith intention to reach settlement, to take at least the preliminary steps they recommend in moving toward that goal.

Opening the Formal Session

Whatever the relationship between the spokespersons, the relationship between the teams may be quite different. If this is a first negotiation or mediation, a cooperative and cordial relationship between employer and employees may have been replaced by chilled formality and even hostility. If it is an established collective bargaining relationship, the parties, despite the impasse, may view the dispute as a temporary aberration in an otherwise good relationship and be eager for help in eliminating the problem. But whether the prenegotiation relationship is new or old, the adversarial nature of the participants' roles and the tensions of the direct negotiations are likely to have added a measure of personal discord that is unrelated to the substance of the issues in dispute.

The atmosphere at the first meeting is often set by the mediator. Arriving at or a trifle after the scheduled time is probably wise, for too early an arrival may produce an uncomfortable situation for the mediator if only one party is present, particularly if the session is in the offices of the employer or the union. Such early encounters are certainly devoid of any wrong, and the mediator can readily avoid any compromising exchange. Yet even the perception of impropriety on the part of the later arriving team might cause problems for the mediator later on. This is particularly true if the parties are familiar with the firm rule of abstention from contacts with a grievance arbitrator. By coming a couple of minutes late to the opening mediation session, the mediator gives the parties an opportunity to mingle and relax a bit. It also provides an opportunity for the spokespersons to chat about the case and, if one or both are new to the case, to clarify the issues or even edge a little toward settlement.

Joint or Separate First Session

Sometimes on arrival the mediator may find the teams in two different rooms. Some mediators leave them separate and begin the mediation by meeting with only one team. If this is the case the mediator will go over the ground rules, but the focus will be on an exposition of the issues in dispute. The proponents of this approach assert that it avoids the hostility and flareups from the opposing party that may mark a joint session, that it provides an opportunity for the team to make a clear, orderly exposition of its view of the impasse and thus remove much of the team's frustration at the lack of movement, and that it builds an image of the mediator as a good listener. They argue further that it provides the mediator with a greater opportunity to challenge positions and propose alternatives and to determine the team's priorities than would be possible in a joint session.

Opponents of this approach argue that it provides only a partisan view of the facts and issues and that rebuttal proposals made by the other side may be ignored. This is particularly so, it is asserted, if the mediator enters into discussion with the team, or offers suggestions for modification of the team's proposals and then relays them to the other side. Having done this, the mediator may be viewed as a deal-maker or an advocate for that team, and may therefore be less acceptable and useful as a neutral orchestrator of the settlement.

The potential for diminished acceptability, and perhaps effectiveness, prompts most mediators to start off the mediation by bringing both teams into one room at the outset. Supporters of this view give the following reasons for including both teams: First, a joint opening session avoids repetition of the opening comments concerning the ground rules for the upcoming mediation and other matters. Second, it assures each side that the mediator is saying the same things to both. Third, it provides the mediator with a vital opportunity to assess the teams and parties' interrelationship; the mediator's approach may be quite different if the relationship is good-natured with pleasant banter and some warmth, than if cold, steely stares with minimal communication across the table are the order of the day. Fourth, it assures that when the time comes for listing of the issues in dispute, each side will hear the other side's full agenda and reactions to its own agenda. It may be that the teams realize they are not apart on some of the issues, or that a listing and interpretation of an issue by one side will prove acceptable by the other side.

To start out meeting with one side alone risks the omission of proposals made by the other side and tends to give the mediator a one-sided view of the conflict. Yet it must be admitted that insisting upon a joint initial session in the face of great hostility may prove to be a mistake, in that it may cause the relationship to deteriorate even further.

Meeting the Team Members

The mediator must recognize that membership on the negotiating team is an achievement and mark of recognition by fellow employees on the union side or by the employer on the management side. Team members are generally proud of their role and conscious of the responsibility associated with team membership and their participation in the mediation. For this reason it is important that the mediator establish as much contact with individual team members as is feasible during the first session. Going around the room shaking hands with each team member and exchanging a few words with each is a good ice breaker, even though it may take a few minutes.

If the teams haven't placed themselves across the table from each other, the mediator usually suggests they do so and then selects a seat at the end of the table closest to the spokespersons. Most mediators then circulate an appearance sheet—a sheet of paper with a line down the center listing the employer and union at the top—and ask the parties to sign on their respective sides. One device that always furthers rapport between people is referring to them by name. If the mediator observes the appearance sheet being passed down one side of the table and then back up the other side, it will be easy to discover who is who from the order in which the sheet was signed on each side. With it in hand it will be possible to assign a name to a face and thus permit identification of team members by name when speaking to them. Some mediators use last names, but my belief is that the process is furthered or perhaps expedited if communication is on a first-name basis. I try to encourage that approach by stating my preference to be addressed by my first name, perhaps with a light remark like "only my wife and children address me as *Mr.* Mediator."

The mediator then should provide a brief introduction—not a dull self-serving resumé but a summary of professional activities, background in mediation, and perception of the mediator's role. It is also the time to set forth any prior agreement as to the mediation schedule; or, if there has been no such agreement, to discuss with the teams the dates and hours for meeting and the point, if any, at which the mediator's involvement in the case must end.

Explaining the Mediator's Role

It is also helpful for the mediator to emphasize that the purpose of the procedure is to help the parties reach *their* agreement, that the mediator has no personal stake in the teams' proposals or what happens to them, does not represent the public interest, will not dictate terms to the parties, and will respect all confidences. It should be emphasized that the mediator will continue the mediation only so long as both sides wish, and that the parties may terminate the mediation and return to direct negotiations at any time.

Mediators usually point out that they have two primary functions. The first is to maintain and if possible improve communications between the parties; to accomplish this the mediator will relay messages and proposals between the parties, meet with the teams and spokespersons separately and jointly, and try to present proposals in the most positive manner to insure a positive reception and reaction.

The second function, to be exercised as the situation warrants, is to serve as a sounding board for altered proposals, to suggest possible alternative wording of proposals and responses to proposals that might make them more palatable, and possibly to make suggestions that will help narrow the differences between the parties.

Some mediators tend to be more aggressive in their mediating role than others. They may warn the teams that on occasion they may come down hard on them, appearing unsympathetic and hostile and attacking the parties' sacred cows and highest priority proposals. They may explain that a negative attitude toward a given proposal may be intended to encourage critical reexamination of the proposal or may reflect indications from the other side that the proposal, if made, will be rejected. They often seek to cushion the impact of such a negative attitude by emphasizing that the other side's proposals will be subject to the same kind of critical analysis.

To maintain decorum and assure a proper focus of authority, the mediator usually will express the preference that there be only one leader per team, although there may be cathartic rewards and a better indication of the dynamics of the situation if the team members are allowed to express themselves from time to time. To avoid too much cross talk, however, the mediator would do well to leave it to each team's spokesperson to designate other team members to speak on a particular issue.

Describing the Format

Since the team members are probably uncertain of their role in dealings with the mediator, the mediator will often explain the types of sessions to be held: joint sessions with both teams present; separate meetings with the respective teams; meetings with the spokespersons separately on some occasions, together at other times. These different formats, it will be noted, will be used to relay proposals, to secure responses, and to assess the status of the mediation. The mediator usually will warn that the separate meetings may be lengthy but should be viewed as an effort to persuade one side to move closer to the other side's position. In that sense the mediator represents the absent side at team caucuses. It is also important to stress that the mediator does not dictate results or serve as a back-up team leader, but works within the structure the parties have created.

This explanation of what is to occur should help to put the participants at ease, and at the same time enhance their trust in the mediator.

Frequently there will be discussion of other ground rules with the parties if the spokespersons have not already worked them out. Among the items on which agreement may be sought are the role of outsiders, press relations, the duration of each day's session, the release of union team members from their regular duties, and access to top managerial personnel who are not present.

Positions of the Parties

Once the ground rules have been established and accepted, it is time to get to the substance of the dispute. As pointed out earlier, it saves time and conflict between the teams if the team leaders are able to agree on the issues to be mediated. Ideally, this will have been completed by a meeting between the spokespersons or in the preliminary session with the mediator. But if there has been no clear agreement on the remaining issues, their status must be clarified by the parties at the first joint session. As may be imagined, the determination of the status of the remaining issues in the presence of the two teams may bring a seemingly routine matter to a fever pitch because of the vested interests of team members in proposals that must now be classified as withdrawn, accepted, tentatively agreed upon, or still on the table. For the team member who had to swallow hard in surrendering a position for a less favorable tentative agreement, this is a logical time to seek a second bite at the apple by urging the team leader not to abandon the position. Each note that is passed is a potential reason for a team caucus, if only for the spokesperson to get his troops back in line. The likelihood of conflict over the classification of issues is increased by the fact that this constitutes the team's first active participation in the mediation. It thus precipitates a game of assertiveness—if only the assertion of the right to caucus and to maintain positions in an effort to intimidate the other side in preparation for the coming gamesmanship of the mediation sessions.

Present Position or Background?

Some parties believe that mediators want to have all the background information on the parties' positions and how they got there—their intermediate proposals, their financial and comparability data, and the like. This belief stems from a view of mediators as decision makers; overlooked is the fact that mediators are not likely to get into such background material, and need not assess the wisdom or failings of the respective positions. Nor are they concerned with how far one or both parties have moved from their opening postures. They are there only to assist the parties in reaching a settlement that they themselves deem acceptable. Therefore, mediators really need only the prior agreement between the parties and knowledge of their current positions at the breakdown in direct negotiations. Mediators' need for data beyond the parties' positions is minimal unless the parties request a ruling or recommendation on some disputed question, as, for example, the legality of a particular proposal. If that occurs, the parties are really asking for arbitration and must supply the information needed for an arbitrator's decision—assuming, that is, that the mediator is willing to act in that capacity.

Arguments on Positions

After hearing the spokespersons express their views of the unresolved issues and clarify any conflict over what is to be mediated, it is prudent for the mediator to read the list back to them to verify what is open. The mediator may then ask the spokespersons if they wish to make an oral argument in the presence of the other side in support of their overall rationale, or to list priorities, or to ask any questions they might have about the procedures.

Some mediators ask for a short statement of the parties' views on each of the outstanding issues. While usually welcomed by the teams as an opportunity for a last chance for each team to convince the other side of the "correctness" of their view on these issues, such a procedure lengthens the session and results in the reiteration of explanations already well known to the other side. Such expositions may be offered on the entire position of the side or, preferably, on an issue-by-issue basis, with each side stating its position on one issue before taking up the next. The latter approach tends to highlight the differences between the parties on each issue. By the manner in which the presentations are made, the mediator and an alert spokesperson can often get a sense of what is important. "This is a must," "Our position for now . . .," "We would like this," etc. Such statements when coupled with the speaker's body language may provide valuable clues as to the approach the mediator should take. They also may afford the mediator at a later stage, when a proposal is under discussion, the opportunity to note, "You heard what they said to that. They won't agree to it."

Apart from these considerations, such expositions serve little purpose. They subject mediators to the respective parties' rationales and invite responses and rebuttals all geared toward persuading the mediator (rather than the opposing side, which has already heard them). The assumptions are, first, that the mediator will be influenced and, being won over, will endeavor to impose his own standards of what is right upon the parties; and second, that mediation is a forum where the mediator will decide what is best for the parties. Such assumptions, if correct, would undermine the basic precept that the mediation belongs to the parties alone and that they should recognize they are engaged in mediation rather than fact finding.

The mediator may take one of two postures during the parties' presentations. The first is to remain silent, interrupting only to ask questions, waiting until the first separate meeting with a team to begin efforts at fostering movement. This role permits the parties to get up to speed in their handling of the issues while giving the mediator a chance to observe the parties and their relationship. It also gives the mediator an opportunity to reflect on the positions the parties have taken while developing a strategy for dealing with those issues once the sessions have begun with the respective teams.

The other posture available to the mediator is a much more active one. Rather than sitting pensively during the parties' presentations, the mediator playing an active role will engage in some parry and thrust during the presentations, endeavoring to poke some holes in both sides' balloons. Although such an approach may pique both teams, it puts them on their toes by challenging some of their assumptions. It also tends to enhance the mediator's credibility and independence by demonstrating an awareness of the extreme nature of certain demands. That it may also prove embarrassing to some of the participants is a price that must be paid.

Challenging Positions

It is the mediator's function to create doubts about the parties' proposals, for that is essential to the rethinking of the merits of both sides' positions. It is such rethinking that leads intelligent negotiators to revise their positions and move toward the compromise and accommodation of which, ultimately, settlements are made.

The mediator's barbs may be uttered in an inoffensive manner to elicit the desired changes in posture. Only a clarification of a proposal may be sought—but this may stimulate a rethinking. "Would your proposal for bereavement leave for death of a family member cover cousins as well?" If able to do this gracefully, without intimidating or embarrassing either side, the mediator may already have launched the mediation effort, in the presence of both teams. This approach, if done in the context of a prior relationship between the mediator and the parties or when there is a measure of camaraderie between the parties, may help to dispose of some minor or ancillary matters while at the same time creating the momentum that is so important for further movement.

Efforts to stimulate movement at the table can be effective only if the spokespersons have the requisite authority to adjust their teams' respective positions. If a team is sufficiently prepared prior to the mediation, it may already have agreed to fall-back positions; the spokespersons can retreat to these without the need for lengthy caucuses, perhaps only with a nod from other team members. If the spokesperson is also the focus of power within the team, he or she may exercise that authority unilaterally by revising a position even without team consultation.

If the spokesperson lacks the authority; however, or if the team has not anticipated the mediator's challenge, the development of a response may require a hurried caucus at the table, or a request for an opportunity for the team to caucus elsewhere. Such interruptions are undesirable at this stage because they disrupt the flow of the parties' presentations, but they may be unavoidable if the mediator undertakes a parry-and-thrust strategy.

Whom to Meet With First

By the close of the first joint session the mediator must determine which side to meet with first. Obviously there are but two choices, but there are multiple considerations in making that choice.

The mediator may opt to meet first with the party that declared the impasse on the theory that that party broke off direct bargaining and should be heard on why it did so. If the meeting with that party's team discloses a superficial reason or a misunderstanding, the mediator may conclude that entry into the dispute was premature and unwarranted, at least at that time, and return the parties to direct negotiations.

The mediator may opt instead to meet with the party proposing the changes in the status quo, as in an arbitration hearing. That side, in a sense, has the burden of proving, to the other side at least, that the existing wages, hours, and/or working conditions should be changed. Traditionally it has been the union, as the party wishing to change the current contract, that occupies that position. In the past few years, however, employers too have taken to proposing substantial contract changes, including costly "give backs." So while the unions continue to propose the greater number of contract changes, it is no longer a one-way street, and it may be difficult for the mediator to determine which party is in fact the moving party.

In a case where the one party has remained adamant in its posture for a period of time in direct negotiations, it makes sense for the mediator to meet with that party first. To meet with the pliant side might be expected to elicit little more than pleas to get the other side to move. The mediator must make the inflexible party aware of the consequences of continued inflexibility if the other side does not come to agree with its position, and must determine whether it is possible to induce some adjustment in the fixed position or at least learn the reason for the inflexibility. If the mediator is persuaded that more movement will *not* be forthcoming, it may be preferable to go to the pliant side to explain the rigidity and determine whether additional surrender of position by that side is feasible.

Another basis for choice of side might be the mediator's perception that personalities rather than issues are the chief stumbling block. If the mediator believes that a belligerent attitude or expression of position underlies the parties' stalemate, it might be worthwhile to meet first with the team and/or team leader that appears to be taking the more antagonistic stance. Such a stance may be either the cause of the other side's obduracy or the effect of the other side's failure to move earlier. To determine which is the case it is imperative that the mediator make an assessment of the reason for the hostility. Only after that assessment will the mediator know whether it is necessary to diffuse the bitterness in order to get the other side to move or, alternatively, to get the other side to move in order to reduce the bitterness.

If the parties know that the mediator has had prior dealings with one of the parties but not the other, the mediator would be wise to meet with the new party in order to overcome any suspicions of partiality. This would also provide the mediator with an opportunity to discuss in greater detail the new party's attitude toward the mediation process.

Yet another basis for choice is provided where one of the parties appears to be ill at ease or insecure in the joint session. To meet with that party's team first offers an opportunity to explain procedures in more detail and to put team members at ease as to what will happen during the mediation. Failing to resolve a team's doubts at the outset might raise its insecurity level to the point where there can be no substantive movement in the mediation.

A final option for the mediator is simply to stay in the joint session room with the team that will be using it as a caucus room. This seemingly casual approach may indicate to the parties that it really doesn't matter to the mediator which group is first at bat. If it is an absolute toss-up, remaining in the same room may be a reasonable course of conduct. But it is likely that each team will assume the mediator has ulterior motives in any case. This being so, the mediator should not permit lethargy to guide him but should decide whom to meet with first on the basis of such factors as those discussed above.

Note Taking

In this initial session, as throughout the mediation procedure, crucial things are said—and even more important things implied—by the participants. Some mediators are adept at remembering almost verbatim what was said to them in caucus. Other mediators confine their note-taking to a few crucial words scribbled on the back of an envelope. But others, including the author, feel much more comfortable with pen and pad at the ready.

Obviously, extensive note-taking is not nearly as important to the mediator as it is to the arbitrator. But fairly frequent note-taking tends to stimulate more careful presentation on the part of the team leaders. Perhaps more important, it permits the mediator to write out verbatim any vital comment or altered proposal without alarming the speaker. Having the exact wording of a statement may become crucial at a later stage of the mediation, especially if a team leader seeks to disavow an earlier statement. When a specific proposal is made, I find it convenient to write down what was said and read it back to the speaker to verify my accuracy.

My procedure for note-taking follows the format described in Chapter 5 for setting forth the positions of the parties, that is, the present contract provision is taped to the top middle of the page, with the proposal of the union to the left and the proposal of the employer to the right, and each proposal or section is given its own page, with tab markers to permit me to find an issue quickly. Notes relating to union statements are placed on the left side of the page under the appropriate proposal, and notes relating to management statements, on the right side. The times at which the notes are taken also are listed. Since it is a common practice to go between caucuses or the parties' spokespersons on one issue at a time, the time sequence gives me the order in which the presentations and comments were made. Even if there is a change of topics and entries are made on another page, the time sequencing will give me the order in which proposals or counterproposals have been made. I use arrows to indicate those items I wish to relay to the other side and place circles around items given to me in confidence. This process permits me to report to the other side any new proposal or position of the party from which I have just come, and is far more accurate than my mental recollection, particularly since I will have read the proposal to the other group before leaving it. Then when I have reported the new information to the party I have just joined, I put a check and time entry next to the arrow from the note reported and go on with my note-taking.

If a proposal involves a number of issues, I will enter the various segments on the respective pages devoted to those issues. I also try to keep a master list at the front of the loose-leaf notebook on which I list a chronology of what is being relayed back and forth and when. Some mediators keep an additional inventory list of all disputed items, checking them off when resolved. The tabs on the pages of my book serve me adequately in that regard.

This plan may entail a lot of page turning and thumbing through the volume, but it results in an up-to-date log showing where the parties stand on the various issues. And if there is any disagreement as to what was reported or proposed, or what the response was, I have a credible chronology of the entire proceedings. This is especially useful if, as often happens, one of the parties asks me to read the notes of what I reported to them in an earlier session.

I circle anything said to me in confidence, and I do not report it to the other side without specific authorization to do so. Personal reactions to proposals and notes to myself on where I think discussions are heading are recorded in a box in the middle of the page. This tells me that these are personal notations, not reported to either side. I similarly place a box around any question I wish to have answered or clarified by either team.

When an issue is disposed of by withdrawal, concession, or compromise, I note the final resolution on the bottom line in the middle of the page devoted to that issue and write "TA" ("tentative agreement") on either side of it. I then take the page from its assigned space and joyfully place it at the back of the book, behind a divider tab, as an issue resolved. This gives me an accurate count of the issues still outstanding as they dwindle in number.

On more than one occasion this system has been used during the mediation to reestablish an agreement when one or both parties disputed the content of an earlier tentative agreement. I have found that my rather routine note-taking has given the parties confidence in my notes, making them the standard for settling disputes over what has been agreed to in the course of the mediation and when.

Confidentiality of Notes

Naturally the book is highly confidential and is kept with me at all times. On occasion, however, I do permit the parties to glance at my book to get a visual sense of where we are, or to recheck the wording of a particular proposal. Like most mediators, I dispose of my notes after the mediation so that if an issue arises years later on one party's intent, I can honestly say, "Sorry, I don't keep my mediation notes."

Summary

The first joint session may not appear to advance the dispute settlement process very much. Its purpose is primarily to expand the process to the parties and to determine their positions on the unresolved positions. It may seem to be merely a rubber stamp of the initial discussions between the spokespersons and the mediator. It may accomplish little more than the formal introduction of participants and issues. Perhaps this could occur just as readily over the telephone or by mail or in the initial separate sessions. Obviously the two sides know each other and where each stands—that is why they are in mediation.

Yet a tone is established in the initial session. The spokespersons in recapitulating their positions have a new audience, the mediator, in addition to an old adversary, the opposing side. Both sides anticipate action, movement, and compromise. The arrival of the mediator has created a new forum—signs, innuendos, body language, and things said and omitted all escalate in this session. The experienced mediator senses the unspoken and encourages the necessary movement by probes and silence. All of this is done in the presence of both teams, so the subtle messages of the mediator are being aimed at the right target—both teams.

The words of give and take may not have been uttered, but the mediation process is nonetheless under way.

7

THE INITIAL SEPARATE MEETING

In the first joint session the mediator is the new arrival in an arena where the contestants have formed their battle lines. No matter how cordial and cooperative the parties might have been before the negotiations, and no matter how compatible the adversaries may appear to be while engaged in small talk in that opening joint session, the parties know the battles lines are drawn. There is bound to be an undercurrent of tension, frustration, or hostility arising from the refusal of both sides to recognize the good sense of the other's position.

The Partisan View of the Mediator

Each side has looked forward to the arrival of the mediator, who, it is hoped, will help persuade the other side of the validity of its proposals. Yet in the joint session the mediator's efforts to establish ground rules and limit presentations to the open issues may jolt each side's perception of the mediator as *its* vehicle for getting the other side to move. The mediator, after all, is a neutral, and in seeking to bring the parties into agreement on the ground rules and the listing of open issues undoubtedly has exerted some pressure.

This impartiality and coaxing may have been expected by the spokespersons because of their prior experience with this or other mediators. It may even have been recognized as necessary to facilitate the proceedings and as an aid in bringing each side's recalcitrant team members into compliance with the mediation format. But it may not have been as well received by the team members, particularly those new to mediation. Those whose pet procedural views were squelched in the discussion of ground rules may also have become skeptical of the process—and even more so of the mediator. There may be disappointment at the mediator's even-handedness.

Team members may view this initial chance to meet with the mediator alone, without the presence and distracting influence of the other side, as their chance to win the mediator over to their position on the issues in dispute. Unable to persuade the other party in direct negotiations, they may view the mediator as a sales agent who will put across proposals that earlier had been rebuffed. The intense conviction usually held by some team members tends to overcome their rational perception in the joint session that the mediator is merely a communicator for both rather than a sales agent for either.

Mediator's View of the Separate Session

The mediator views the separate team session as an opportunity to establish or reestablish standing with the team. It is the mediator's chance to gain the confidence of the team members.

The session with a single team provides an opportunity for freer discussion, for the mediator to gain insight into the problems existing between the parties, and for the parties to become aware that the mediator understands their problems at least enough to help to solve them through the mediation process. Much can be said for the cathartic benefits of having the mediator available as a concerned listener to hear team members pour out their frustrations. Among the most frequently heard accolades about "good" mediators is that they listen, they don't pontificate, and they don't pass judgment upon the participants and their positions until requested to do so.

Once the mediator has closed out the joint session by designating a team to meet with, it may be helpful to give that team a few minutes alone to review its strategy and prepare its presentation.

Opening the Team Session

The mediators must be aware of the need to win the team's confidence. This is important not merely to get the team to reveal its fall-back positions or bottom line. It is important also to achieve an atmosphere of receptivity when the mediator comes in with a proposal from the other side. If the team wishes the mediator to be its agent for trying to sell a proposal to the other party, it should be willing to listen to the mediator's report of what the other side can give and what it needs to get.

Winning and, more important, keeping a team's confidence is a delicate matter. It begins when the mediator enters the room. If the joint session has been fiery, with the animosity of the other side strongly in evidence, a good beginning is a shake of the head, a sigh or "whew," or the words, "Wow, I can see why you reached impasse!" It can help to take off one's jacket and roll up one's sleeves. Even choosing a seat on one side of the table rather than at the head, as an arbitrator would, sends a message and tends to encourage the team to accept the mediator as "one of us."

It is advisable to steer clear of the issues at the outset and spend some time in small talk, asking about the background of the team members, their constituencies, how many have been in negotiations and/or mediation before, what their regular work is, and the like. It often helps to ask whether anyone has questions about the procedure or anything that came up in the joint session, or, if asked, to talk some more about the mediator's role, or one's own background.

These few minutes spent having a cup of coffee and chatting before launching into the substance of the dispute can prove to be a worthwhile investment in building trust between the team and the mediator. It also provides a means of erasing any impression of the mediator as harsh, aggressive, or aloof that might have been gained prior to the mediation or from the mediator's conduct in the joint session.

One mediator has stated to me that he deliberately gives the impression of being a tough guy in the joint session and then changes his approach in the initial separate first sessions by taking a much more sympathetic and considerate approach. He believes this devious tactic not only wins support and confidence but also instills a little guilt in the team for having misjudged him as a "heavy."

One of the techniques often used by mediators to inspire confidence is to stress the desirability of a settlement, the mediator's commitment to securing only a settlement that is acceptable to the team, and the mediator's need for help from the team in moving toward that goal. The mediator is, of course, powerless to effect a settlement on his own. The power to settle is within the sole authority of the parties. The mediator, in order to stimulate movement to bring the parties together, must have the support and confidence of both teams. This confidence can be so complete that the parties may openly admit which positions are firm, which are flexible, and which are throwaways.

Accrediting the Spokesperson

While seeking to communicate with the team members, the mediator must also be sensitive to the need of the team's leader. It is not wise to let the team members feel too close to the mediator or to feel they have the right to deal with him directly beyond the initial exploration of their attitudes, for too ready access to the mediator unquestionably undercuts the authority of the spokesperson. Since the spokesperson presumably has been selected for his or her leadership qualities, it is important to reinforce the leader's position from time to time. When the mediator later is endeavoring to get the team to modify positions it earlier deemed sacred, a strong team leader may be the difference between success and failure. After the initial ice-breaking it might be appropriate, therefore, for the mediator to turn to the spokesperson to ask for a recitation of the problems as the team sees them. This shifting of the focus to the spokesperson shows the mediator as a person willing to share the limelight and responsibility; and tends to enhance the prestige of the spokesperson as both the link to the mediator and the recognized locus of the team's authority. The leader is certainly more familiar than the mediator with the issues in dispute and with the internal politics of his own team—if not of both teams. He or she is probably the best person to set forth the team's rationale for its proposals and to determine the order in which issues should be presented.

The mediator should be aware, however, that the leader may be too closely identified with the team's position to advise the mediator objectively on what is needed to get to settlement. Some spokespersons are independent professionals eager to resolve the dispute and move on. But others are hired guns who consider it their duty to fight as long as the team wishes before switching gears and altering their position. There are also those who have been identified with the team for so long that they have become prejudiced, programmed champions and "true believers" of their client's cause; such persons may be the most difficult to deal with.

The mediator must be careful not to become captive of the ideologies on either side. The spokesperson must be allowed to make the presentation, analysis, and prognosis that are politically necessary. The information these provide is essential to the mediator in the continuing assessment of the participants and the effort to move them toward settlement. But the mediator must retain the right to pull in the reins if the spokesperson's personal commitments begin to hinder rather than help the mediation process.

Explaining the Position

Mediators differ in the extent to which they permit or encourage detailed presentations by the parties of their positions on the issues in dispute. One group takes the view that such presentations take too much time and are more suited to the arbitration forum than to mediation. Proponents of this view point to the joint opening session as the appropriate forum for identifying the issues, particularly because of the opportunity it provides for rebuttal and for sharpening the issues; their preference is to use the first separate session to begin seeking position modifications.

Proponents of the other view hold that detailed presentations, possibly including the negotiating history, meet the team's need to have its views fully heard by the mediator and that prohibiting them forces team members to conclude that the mediator really doesn't care about the work problems that underlie their position. The extra time spent in listening at this point, they believe, will pay off later in the mediation in the form of willingness on the part of the team to respond to a bid to alter a position because it knows the mediator is aware of the reasons for it. The most persuasive argument for permitting detailed presentations is that they provide the mediator with a window on the team's thinking. The order of presentation, the lumping of proposals, the intensity or casualness of presentation, and the designation of a strong or weak team member to speak on a particular topic are all prominent signals that help the mediator in assessing the strengths and weaknesses and determining the priorities of the teams.

For the spokesperson to begin with an issue as the team's No. 1 priority certainly means more than listing it at the end of a presentation as one of "the remaining items we need" . . . or "want" or "would like." Certainly the message is made explicit when the leader turns to a team member and directs, "Why don't you tell the mediator about the proposal you want?"; or "Tell us about the proposal that came out of that grievance you lost last year."

The Mediator's Reaction

Obviously the signals are usually much more subtle, but to experienced mediators the ordering and method of presentation of positions—what is said and what is omitted—can often provide a loud and clear message of the team's (or leader's) commitment to the various issues. Careful and sustained listening throughout is essential. Cross examination or criticism may do as much harm as personal endorsement of a position. Any expression of approval of or opposition to a proposal may well come back to haunt the mediator. He may be accused of having scuttled a proposal to which he took exception or of having "failed" as a mediator because a proposal previously embraced as "desirable" is not accepted by the other side.

Yet being a good listener and avoiding debate does not mean the mediator must remain silent during such presentations. The mediator is aware that positions and proposals relayed to the other side will be rejected or at least challenged. In anticipation of this it is wise to seek any needed clarifications. Questions seeking clarification, of course, can be aimed at modifying proposals slightly to make them more palatable. The mediator can do this in a very supportive way without taking sides on any proposal. An example might be a question such as this: ''What if they object to the number of days in your leave proposal?'' Mediators must, however, be careful to avoid excessive input—a particular temptation when meeting with an inexperienced team. They must remember that they were not hired by both parties to be an advocate for one.

Probing of this kind may not achieve immediate movement, but it sets the stage for the reexamination and possible alteration of proposals at a later stage of the mediation. It is important that the mediator be able to instill doubts in each team about the survivability of the proposals to which they adhere so doggedly. Yet the mediator must be careful not to become—or even give the impression of becoming—a proponent or advocate of a particular proposal or viewpoint. Should this happen, the parties both will find themselves engaged in negotiations with the mediator, and the settlement will be crafted by the mediator rather than the parties.

Assessing the Team

One of the most troublesome tasks for the mediator in the initial meeting with each team is to assess the team membership and the relationship of the spokesperson to the team. This is important not only to determine whether the leader really can speak for the team, but whether there is a power center elsewhere in the team. It may become a crucial matter later in the mediation. If the initial assessment is that the leader is indeed the power center of the team, separate meetings with that person later on may prove to be fruitful. If, on the other hand, the leader is no more than a mouthpiece for team members, an early assessment of that fact permits the mediator to avoid fruitless sessions with a powerless person. If the assessment shows that one of the team members rather than the leader is the power center, then it might be fruitful for the mediator to try to contrive to meet with that person in caucuses, with or without the nominal leader. For example, the mediator might propose at the appropriate time that each side be represented in caucuses by the spokesperson and one other person, perhaps specifying who the others should be.

These assessments of the authority and competence of the spokesperson may not be completed in the initial meeting. It is the opening session with a team, however, that provides the first chance to assess the power distribution as well as the team constituencies. It may well turn out that the power center moves among the team members depending on the issue on the table. Thus, in a teacher dispute, the spokesperson may come from the state teacher group. If that group is subsidizing the local body, the state representative may indeed be the power center on some or all of the issues and in particular on the compensation package. A leader who is the president of the local may have a powerful electoral base. Yet the power even of a person in that position may depend on when the term of office ends, whether there is an opposition leader, or whether an opposition union is waiting in the wings.

The movement of the power center may depend on the issue and the strength of the constituency. If school nurses are part of the bargaining unit, their demand for parity between their salaries and those of teachers might seem to have minimal support, since meeting the demand would presumably take money from the pockets of the classroom teachers. But if the number of nurses was large or if the nurses played a crucial role in the election of the incumbent leadership, the demand might have strong support from the leadership. More dramatic may be the presence of an athletic coach on the negotiating team. The coach might have little impact on most issues, but when the discussion focused on extracurricular or coaching stipends the coach's constituency might extend beyond sports to encompass all teachers engaged in extra-curricular activities. Indeed, the constituency on that issue might even spill over to sports enthusiasts, parents of athletes, and town boosters on the management side.

Years of mediating have taught the author that the composition of management and union teams tends to be similar from one negotiation to the next. The union usually has its militants who favor holding firm "at any cost," as well as its milquetoasts who are reluctant to speak out or rock the boat. The management team usually has its cost-conscious members who care little for the tranquility that concessions could buy, and a certain number of anti-union members. A member of the team representing a school board in my first mediation, an office clerical who vowed, "No teacher is going to make more money than I do," has been in attendance in one guise or another at every mediation since. So too has been the union team member who declared, "They don't realize they're being stubborn. Tell them to give in."

Impressions of the Spokesperson's Authority

The actions of the spokespersons, the manner and extent of their deferral to other team members for the presentation of particular issues, their tolerance of discussion or dissent, and the way in which they are able to maintain control of the diverse constituency making up the team may be very important to the mediator. The assessment may not be based on words alone. If the leader is continually being handed notes by the team members, it may signal a lack of control. If the notes consistently come from a single team member, it may indicate that the member is the power center, or a spoiler. Whether this is so may be inferred from the spokesperson's reaction to the notes. Do they lead to adjustments in position? Do they result in conferences with the note writer, interrupting the presentation? Are they ignored while the leader plods ahead, oblivious to attempts to alter the presentation? Does the leader scowl at the note writer, or assign another team member to deal with that person? Does the spokesperson tolerate whispering or outbursts by team members? How are objections dealt with?

Assessing the Proposals

Another of the mediator's key objectives at the initial meeting with a team is to determine the relative importance of the various proposals. Which are the most important issues? Which can be sacrificed in the interest of compromise? And which are there as bargaining chips, to be readily traded or withdrawn for benefits in other areas?

The nurses' proposed inclusion on the teachers' salary schedule, for instance, may be an important team issue, or it may have been included on the list of demands to placate the nurses, ready to be withdrawn for a concession from the other side. The same may be true of the proposed increase in extracurricular stipends. The mediator makes an assessment of the relative importance of these and other issues not only from the language of the proposals, the presentation of the spokesperson, and the reaction of the team member representing that constituency, but also from prior experience with teacher negotiations. Prior experience indicates that in a large school system there may be a substantial number of nurses, but not enough to overturn a settlement. At the same time, the mediator knows that an increase in the extracurricular stipend will affect a much larger fraction of the teacher group, particularly in a relatively small school system where the majority of the ratifying body may be engaged in one or more such activities. The majority of that unit might prefer an increase in the stipend to the same amount of money distributed throughout the system as part of a general salary improvement package.

The mediator may also know from prior mediating efforts elsewhere that a proposal with seemingly minimal support is in fact an objective of a strong national or state-wide organization that is hoping for a breakthrough in this negotiation. Self-funding of medical insurance or attainment of dental and eye-care insurance coverage are two such subjects that have been pushed recently as part of larger state or national bargaining agendas by employers or unions.

Insights of this kind may be a product of prior experience or of keen assessment of the presentation of the team during the initial session. Identifying the political issues and their champions on the team may be very important to the mediator in later efforts to get the parties to focus on the issues that are most important to their respective constituencies and the issues that will bring settlement.

Assessing the Other Team

The initial team sessions also provide the mediator with an opportunity to gain some insight into the composition of the other team. When the two teams have had a relationship at the workplace over the years and have been debating a settlement across the bargaining table for months, it is relatively simple to secure an assessment of the other team. An expression of even minimal interest in the subject by the mediator is usually enough to bring an outpouring of detail about each member of the other team.

Such information can be of value to the mediator as he seeks to determine how the power and responsibility are distributed among the members of the other team. But in evaluating that information the mediator must be mindful of the source, and must be prepared to shut off the flow of negative comments if they exceed the bounds of good taste and decorum.

The Forecast

A source of help to the mediator in plotting strategy for the mediation is the "best-case scenario" perception of each team. The mediator may have secured some enlightenment in the preliminary session with the spokespersons prior to the first joint meeting. But if that session did not enable the mediator to develop a strategy for securing a settlement, it is important that the task of doing so be undertaken in the first separate sessions with the teams.

Each team obviously has an "ideal scenario" leading to triumph in the mediation. It may be willing to disclose this scenario to the mediator, who will thereby be able to form a picture of the team's strategy in the mediation. The process of spelling out the team's hoped-for resolution may prove to be helpful to team members as well as to the mediator. It gives the mediator a chance to elicit clarifications of the team's objectives and may also stimulate some rethinking of positions. The mediator may also secure a more accurate assessment of the team's priorities than a mere request would provide.

Obtaining a best-case scenario from each team provides the mediator with an ongoing and up-to-date picture of what each team is trying to achieve, its view of the other side's proposals and of the other side's reaction to its proposals, and the prospects for alteration of its position. Fortunate is the mediator who secures an honest projection from each team. But that mediator is burdened as well, and must exercise additional care in both camps, first to avoid disclosing his knowledge of fall-back positions and second to avoid disclosing the strategy of one side to the other.

Determining Priorities

Even with the perceptions gained from best-case scenarios, the mediator should still probe to determine each team's priorities. The mediator need not be a silent observer in this effort, and can ask the team directly to state its priorities. Which items are needed most? Which can be dropped or postponed until another negotiation? The mediator need not be so naive as to expect honest answers to such questioning early in the proceedings, or perhaps ever. The spokesperson must be recognized as a political animal who is negotiating with the mediator to have the most formidable case presented to the other side. So statements about priorities, particularly at the outset, will probably not be completely candid. They will probably identify the real objectives, but they will also include other items that the leader wants the other team to believe are priorities, on the theory that, if they cannot be attained, at the very least a substantial price can be exacted for their withdrawal. If questioning is done in the presence of team members, the list may also include some of the favorite proposals of powerful or troublesome team members. Eventually such proposals may fall by the wayside, but for the time being they must be treated as issues of priority.

Perhaps more revealing is a team's perception of the other side's priorities. Sometimes that perception may be wishful thinking, but if the parties have been engaged in sufficiently intense negotiations prior to the mediation, a team may be able to provide a rather accurate picture of what the other side really is after.

Mediators differ as to the pressure that should be exerted to persuade each side to list its priorities. Some make a determined effort in the initial separate session to identify the elements that are of critical importance to the team. They then present a package containing these elements to the other side and seek to forge a compromise. Implicit in this approach is the abandonment of proposals not on the initial priority list. Such proposals, however, may come back to haunt the mediator when a settlement is at hand because, though not of the highest priority, they nevertheless are of substantial importance to one team or the other.

A less dramatic way of eliciting the true priorities is to watch and wait as the teams formulate their proposals and their responses. By paying close attention to these formulations and to the way in which the initial statements of position and team forecasts were made, the mediator can often form an accurate picture of team priorities. Such an approach avoids the risk of being provided an inaccurate or deliberately misleading list.

Message Transmission

If the mediator is to be considered a confidant by both teams, information received in confidence during the mediation must not be divulged. Such information might concern a prospective fall-back position, a response that will be forthcoming if a certain concession is made by the other side, or an admission that something that must remain on the table for now may be withdrawn later. Mediators are always privy to such confidential information, and they must take care to see that it remains confidential. To violate the trust placed in him spells the end of the mediator's career, for word soon spreads that he cannot be trusted.

Most mediators follow the practice of treating whatever they hear in a private session with a team as within their discretion to reveal to the other side at the time they deem most propitious. However, if the team wants the mediator to hold certain information in confidence, it should specify when it discloses the information that it is for the mediator's ears only and not to be divulged until such time as it is specifically released for the mediator's use. Mediators can usually be trusted to live up to those conditions; once they show themselves to be trustworthy, the flow of vital, private information is likely to increase, making their mediation task that much easier. When both sides feel able to confide in the mediator, negotiations between the parties can be much more effective. The mediator knows what each side's next step will be, and being privy to the next proposal or counterproposal will be able to handle the mediation process smoothly and rapidly.

Chamber of Horrors

Frequently the initial meeting with one of the individual teams is marked by a strong expression of determination to see the team's total package accepted by the other side. Unique to the public sector seems to be an unwillingness to recognize all the hurdles that must be overcome before full acceptance can be realized. On both the management and the union side there is a tendency to believe that the other side will see the error of its ways and come into the fold, or simply fold.

On the management side there may be a high-minded but tight-fisted determination to hold the line, to increase efficiency, and to make better utilization of the work force, perhaps even with fewer employees. Management is often so persuaded of the wisdom of its position that it forgets the contract bears two signatures, and that the union's agreement is necessary if the hoped-for economies are to occur. It thus may fall to the mediator to point out the need for accommodation and compromise if a team's package proposal is not warmly embraced by the other side. And if compromise is not forthcoming, it may be necessary for the mediator to recite the chamber of horrors that might ensue if management fails to compromise—that there may be no agreement; that an otherwise docile group might be galvanized to militancy; that there might be a strike, a work-to-rule, or "blue flu"; or that any of a number of scenarios might be played out that could backfire on management and bring just the results the employer is seeking to avoid.

It is perhaps even more likely on the union side that the team leader, with team members nodding agreement, will proclaim the inviolability of its position and the determination to go the route to achieve the team's objectives. It is usually the mediator's task to puncture that balloon of self-righteousness. More often than not the problem is with the team rather than with the more experienced leader. "But what if management does not agree? What will you do then?" "And if the fact-finder finds against you, or if the employer does not voluntarily agree to accept the recommendations even if you win at that step? What will you do? Will you strike?" "Will everyone honor the picket line? How many will work?" "How long will it be before some of your members need the money enough to return to work?" "What if an injunction is issued?" "More important, how long will you be able to sustain a strike?" "And if some refuse to strike, or if some return to work, what will happen to your organization?" "Will the rival group gain control?" "How long would you have to stay on strike for the employer to have saved enough money in wages to pay you the increase in compensation that you are striking over. . . how long before you are paying for the increase through your strike?"

Clearly the participants come to the mediation somewhat convinced of the virtue and propriety of their proposals. They tend to minimize the risks associated with fighting to the death to achieve them.

It is in this context that the mediator can perform a very real service by seeking to persuade the teams of the folly of going to the barricades. It must be stressed that a settlement achieved through compromise will secure a return to tranquility without the disruption and animosities that arise and persist in a conflict situation. The chamber-of-horrors speech may be hard for overzealous team members to take, and it may have to be repeated at later steps, but it is one of the most important contributions the mediator can make. It represents an effort to bring a measure of reality to the relationship between the parties, and in the final analysis an expression of the necessity for achieving ultimate agreement.

Closing the Initial Session

At the close of the initial separate session, the mediator should tell the team what the next step will be, i.e., a similar meeting with the other team. It is important that the mediator explain the task facing the team he is leaving. Usually the mediator urges a reassessment of the team's position and a revision of its proposals to make them more palatable to the other side.

The mediator should also announce whether he will return after meeting with the other team or whether the group should seek him out after it has completed its reassessment. Too often nothing is said in this regard, so the team waits anxiously for a mediator who may be in his own room awaiting a call from the team after it has completed reassessing its position.

Summary

The initial separate session with a team provides a chance for the team to gain confidence in the mediator and for the mediator to assess the power, authority, composition, and priorities of the team. Ideally, it leads to a comfortable relationship in which the team will entrust the mediator with its confidences. The achievement of such a relationship with both parties will enable the mediator to move more rapidly toward position modifications and ultimate settlement.

The mediator should begin in these opening sessions to probe the intentions of the team by inquiring of each its forecast of how the mediation will proceed. The mediator should also seek to ascertain the team's priorities and endeavor to persuade the teams of the need for proposal modification and compromise if agreement is to be reached.

8

SELECTING THE FIRST ISSUE

The formalities of the parties getting to know the mediator and of the mediator getting to know the parties may take time, but they are constructive and essential preliminary steps on the road to settlement. There may be some strains and stresses because of the personality differences of the combatants, but generally these obstacles are overcome and the parties and the mediator are able to achieve sufficient rapport to proceed to the substance of the dispute.

Cordiality and day-to-day work relationships between the parties notwithstanding, the dispute into which the mediator has been called or assigned is generally a very real conflict. It usually also involves a perceived need to achieve certain changes in the relationship as a basis for operations between the parties for the life of the forthcoming agreement. If the collective bargaining agreement between the parties is, as some describe it, a treaty between the union and the employer, the fact that their negotiations have led to a deadlock places the mediator in the position of being the one to arrange the truce that precedes the discussion and the final agreement on the terms of that treaty.

In the context of the potential distrust between the parties and the strategies being pursued by each to achieve the agreement most favorable to that side, the sequence of the issues to be discussed or mediated takes on significant dimensions.

Multiplicity of Issues

The debate over whether the teams should bring a large number of issues or a small number of issues to mediation is largely political. If there is hostility in the relationship that extends throughout the work force, or frustration over a cluttered grievance procedure, or a poorly disciplined procedure for reducing the number of demands, or a mediating team whose members have pet issues, the number of issues is likely to be large.

Mediators obviously prefer to mediate in a context where the parties singly as well as jointly have made a sincere effort to reduce the items in dispute to the serious questions they have earnestly tried but failed to resolve. In such a setting there is proof of intent to settle. But when the number of issues is so great that it bespeaks an unwillingness on the part of the teams to reduce the number separately or jointly or, worse, an inability to do so, many mediators will decline to go forward.

On occasion I have received proposals including 400 items for mediation, some with subissues within them. In those situations I point out the futility and cost of mediating all items. I calculate for them the cost for the length of time it will take to spend the bare minimum of one hour on each item multiplied by 400 items, or about eight hours a day for 50 work days. I then calculate the cost of my participation in that process and suggest that, even though each only has to pay half, they will also have their own costs in lost wages and the fees of outsiders to add to that.

The information is jolting. I quietly suggest that the length of the list reflects either refusal to meet and surmount internal political problems or unwillingness to undertake realistic negotiation. The dread I feel over the prospect of coping with such parties and issues leads me to insist that the parties reduce the number of issues to no more than 20 before I'll begin to mediate. That may scare them off, and may indeed provide a couple of months of full time work for whatever mediator they select as a substitute. Generally, however, the parties do respond to the exhortation. They may return later in frustration at having failed to get below 27, but by that time their commitment to movement has been demonstrated and the mediation begins.

Paradoxically, the process of winnowing the list of issues to a manageable size often makes it easy to select the first issue. That problem may be resolved by casually asking, "What were you working on last? Let's see if we can resolve that item first."

Agreed-Upon Agenda

In some cases the parties agree in advance or in caucus on the order in which the unresolved issues are to be discussed. They may already have determined that it is to their mutual advantage to begin with major questions, such as wages or reductions in force, or, on the other hand, with some of the minor issues. The mediator generally cares not what order is followed in discussing the various issues. If the team leaders have worked out a scenario or sequence for attacking the disputed issues, their game plan will usually be acceptable; they know better than the mediator what the shortest road to settlement is.

An agreed-upon agenda may be reached for a very different reason—the parties recognize that their dispute is one that cannot be resolved in mediation, and are just going through the motions. The mediator in that situation will generally accept the parties' conclusion that a normal mediation would be pointless and ineffective. If there is a mutual intent merely to comply with a statutory or contractual requirement that there be a mediation step before they can proceed to fact finding or binding arbitration—or even a strike—the mediator will be unlikely to challenge the spokespersons joint game plan by insisting on proceeding with a mediation that neither party is willing to undertake. The mediator might make some effort to get the parties to abandon their escalating game plan and *try* mediation or endeavor to talk them into some exchanges that might narrow the gap in the hope of triggering mediation. But apart from that, the mediator will go through the formalities necessary to permit an honest certification that mediation has been tried and that the effort failed.

The Typical Case

Except for the two foregoing situations, the mediator can usually expect that there will be a substantial dispute on the order in which issues are to be discussed, and in particular on which item is to be considered initially. Certainly the parties may have good reasons to deal with one issue rather than another first in the mediation. But often the dispute is not on the merits of which issue should be considered first. Rather, the dispute represents the first test of strength between the parties in the mediation. The mediator may thus be faced with a dispute that is more one of form than of substance.

Let us take, for example, a dispute in which management insists that wages be discussed first, while the union insists that greater job protection in the event of layoffs be the first issue. How should the mediator deal with that conflict? One way is to go back and forth between the parties trying to get one side to agree to the other's priority. Each side, of course, recites an extended litany as to why its chosen issue should be tackled first.

Another approach is to seek to combine the two issues, dealing with both at once as a sort of package. This approach is a bit unwieldy as an opening gambit, since the mediator knows little about either issue yet must know enough to be able to construct balanced proposals on each subject to present to each side.

If the parties are adamant about starting with their respective pet issues, the mediator might decline to become the ball in their ping-pong game. One possibility would be to back off until the parties reach a mutual understanding on what is to be the first issue. But ducking that portion of their dispute might be a dereliction of duty on the part of the mediator, because that issue is in fact a crucial element of their deadlock. An alternative would be to suggest a coin toss to select the first issue, explaining that the sequence doesn't matter since all issues will have to be dealt with before there can be a final agreement.

Still another approach is to avoid a choice between the two openers by suggesting that the teams instead commence mediation with some less controversial issue in order to get the ball rolling. The mediator might identify a particular issue as the starter, or propose that the issues be considered in the order in which they are found in the present agreement or the list of issues presented at the opening session. The mediator might even be so arbitrary as to propose considering the issues on the basis of the order in which they were inserted into the issues notebook. In a sense it really does not matter which other issue is taken up first, since the main objective is to break the stalemate between the parties.

Big Issue or Little Issue

But even if the mediator assumes total responsibility for selecting the issue to be taken up first, it still is necessary to decide whether to start with a big issue or a little one. Orchestrating the entire mediation is a critical factor for the mediator. The teams have presented their issues, and the mediator presumably has reflected on them. From those reflections should have come a sense of what is being sought and, from prior experience in this industry and in comparable situations, what is attainable. The mediator, antennae fine tuned from previous battles, frequently can make an accurate assessment of whether or not the dispute is likely to settle in mediation.

The Little Issues

One group of mediators takes the position that the little issues should be first, especially if the prospects for settlement appear good. They reason that movement or compromise is more likely in the case of the little issues because the stakes are not so high. Moreover, there is less pressure and ego involvement on the part of the team members in the case of the little issues, which makes them more susceptible to compromise, trade-off, or withdrawal. If there is movement on these minor issues, the mediator will be able to point to a developing attitude of cooperation, which in turn can lead to movement thereafter on the more important, bigger issues. And, indeed, if there is "victory" on some of the smaller issues, there may be less need for "victory" on the bigger issues. This creates more room for compromise on the bigger issues. And even if movement on the bigger issues it not forthcoming, the argument goes, at least some of the smaller issues have been eliminated. This reduces the total number of issues in dispute, cutting the cost of subsequent fact finding or arbitration and permitting sharper focus in those later forums on the tougher issues that are the main bones of contention.

The Bigger Issues

Another group of mediators takes the view that it is more realistic to hit the bigger issues first, especially if the mediation is foreseen as not coming to a successful completion. Their position is that the parties must confront head-on the need for accommodation on the issues they consider the most important. If there is no movement at all on these issues, there is no point in wasting the mediator's time, or the parties' time and money. If it is certain that the case will proceed to fact finding or arbitration, then all outstanding issues should be available for consideration in the next forum. There should be no reduction in the number of issues to the "crucial" issues, since this would have an adverse impact upon any subsequent efforts to put together a mutually acceptable settlement package. On the other hand, if this approach is successful in achieving settlement of one "big" issue, the teams might be stimulated to move on the remaining issues as well. When the big issues are resolved, say the proponents of this approach, other issues will fall into place or be abandoned along the way.

Speedy Selection of the Opener

Whichever approach the mediator elects to take for a particular dispute, it is desirable that the choice be made expeditiously, without leaving time for discussion between the teams or for second guessing the decision as to which issue should be dealt with first. If challenged, the mediator can simply state: "I think it will be better or smoother if we start with X instead of either of the issues you two are arguing about. Don't worry, we'll get to those issues, too. And there will not be any agreement until you are both satisifed with the outcome of your so-called priority issues. Of course, if you both agree on some other issue we'll start with that one."

If forced to choose between two big issues, each being proposed as the starting point by one of the parties, I prefer to select the one that in my estimation is the greater impediment to settlement. In most cases that is the issue of compensation or availability of funds. I have found that agreement on that issue tends to put other subjects in a different perspective. Thus, if the parties agree to devote a certain amount of money to salaries, that may dispose of a number of other cost items, such as increases in health insurance payments or overtime pay and the like.

Salaries and reductions in force are two issues that are also interrelated. Only if the salary issue is put to rest will it be possible to determine the number of employees who may be subject to layoff. To treat the items in reverse order would lead to disputes over abstract concepts and standards, with the two sides fighting over language appropriate to the large-scale layoff that might be made necessary by a disproportionately large increase in salaries.

Such a strategy can backfire, however. In one community where the union sought to concentrate on minor noneconomic issues while the employer sought to negotiate wages first, the parties were stalemated until they finally agreed to focus on money. After several hours a wage package was agreed upon, and the union sought to turn the discussion to the noneconomic items it had tabled. At that point the employer representative stated, "We will agree to the economic package we have just worked out but will agree to no changes in any contract language." The union at this point was stymied. If it rejected the tentatively agreed-upon economic package to secure noneconomic benefits, it would be unable to get ratification of the ultimate settlement. At the same time, the noneconomic issues were not sufficiently important to gain the membership support needed for a successful strike. And if the employer made it known that an acceptable economic package had been offered and rejected, the union risked the disaffection of its membership.

Boulder in the Road

The parties seldom hassle the mediator on his choice of which issue to proceed with, but there are occasions when one of them will place what mediator Eva Robins has called a "boulder in the road," and refuse to negotiate on any other item until a particular issue is laid to rest. It takes two parties to create a boulder in the road. One insists on discussing and settling a specific issue before considering any other subject, and the other insists on another approach and refusing to commit itself to the resolution of that issue at that time. Generally the parties reach this position after discussing or at least identifying an issue; unable to move forward on it, one of them seeks to table that issue and turn to something else. The first party objects, insisting upon its resolution before anything else is discussed.

The disputed topic may be the primary concern of the party raising it, a concern which if not satisfactorily resolved might indeed lead to rejection of any other proposal for settlement. An example might be the salary package or protection against layoff in a pending personnel reduction situation. To the extent that an issue is of primary concern to both parties, however, both probably will agree to stay with it, avoiding the problem. More often the boulder in the road is a demand for resolution of an issue of much lesser magnitude. Often it is an issue that, if the moving party did not insist on its handling as a precondition for discussion of other issues, might well be washed out or ignored in the process of settling issues of more significance to both parties, such as rectification of an arbitration award or the settlement of a pending grievance that appears to be a loser.

Another example might be the union's insistence on binding arbitration after the employer had refused to implement an earlier arbitration decision favorable to the union. Yet another might be the employer's insistence that the school teachers' contract run until July 15 instead of December 31, in the expectation that such a deadline would be ineffective as a strike date because schools would be closed and teachers dispersed for the summer. In these examples the issue is raised as an impediment, an exaction of ransom for continuation of the negotiations. In itself it is not of such significance that failure to resolve it would preclude a final settlement. Given enough other benefits, the union in the first example would be likely to drop a demand for binding arbitration, since the decision that sparked it might affect only a few employees. Similarly, in the second example the employer probably would agree to retain a December expiration date if that was the only barrier to settlement. In both cases the boulder in the road is an issue that takes on significance not because of its merits but because it stands as a bar to further negotiations on issues of greater significance to both parties.

How is the mediator to deal with the boulder in the road? If unsuccessful in trying to push it off the road to divert attention to more pressing matters, the mediator must find a way to bring it into the mainstream of the negotiations. Take the case of a union's binding arbitration demand. One approach by the mediator eager to move on to salary matters might be to couple the two issues: "Would you be agreeable to excluding salary matters from arbitration?" "The employer will consider limited binding arbitration once the total salary package is agreed to." "Binding arbitration is possible if the salary increase is limited to 4 percent.''

If it is not feasible to join another issue to the boulder, the mediator might try chipping away at the boulder itself: "Would the union agree to limit binding arbitration to discipline and discharge cases?" An alternative is for the other team to come up with its own boulder. Perhaps the boulders can then be traded off or both abandoned, provided each side is willing to expand the discussion to the other side's boulder.

Still another approach might be to ask the party responsible for the boulder what issues it would be willing to surrender in return for agreement upon the disputed demand, or what concessions it thinks the other side would insist upon in exchange for agreeing to that demand. In either case new issues probably would be put on the table for discussion, and the focus of the discussion might actually shift away from the boulder to the trade-off issues. With the emphasis on these other elements of the package, the boulder may disappear. Eva Robins has suggested referring boulders in the road to joint study committees, or going public in cases where there is public interest in the dispute.

It matters little to the mediator whether his choice or the parties' choice of issue is being discussed. What is important to the mediator is that discussions be productive and contribute toward settlement. Thus the challenge of the boulder in the road is not whether the issue in question will be conceded. Perhaps the mediator will be able to talk the other side into agreeing to it. But if unsuccessful in getting one side or the other to yield, the mediator should seek to divert talk from the dead-end confrontation of "you must," "we won't," to the more malleable issues. Only in that way can movement occur.

Unilateral Drops

The general expectancy in mediation, as in direct negotiations, is that one party will alter its position only if the other party does likewise on the same or some other issue. Thus movement by one side is dependent upon prior movement by the other side. This "after you, Alphonse" approach is an easy recipe for deadlock. Certainly the mediator or the parties can ultimately find a triggering change that will touch off a chain reaction of changes, but this frequently requires a lot of frustrating issue exploration and careful packaging.

A different approach undertaken with success by some mediators is to encourage or induce one party, early in the mediation, to make a unilateral change in its position to show its good-faith commitment to the mediation process and its desire to reach a settlement. In trying to talk the party into this course of action, the mediator can look through the issues on the table and usually, from prior experience, spot one that is a "throwaway." It may be possible to persuade the party that throwing it away now may encourage a similar move by the other team. This tactic is of particular value at the outset of the mediation when the parties are still suspicious of each other, and perhaps smarting over the fact that resort to mediation was necessary to get any movement from the other side. A unilateral move helps to engender faith in the process and perhaps also faith in the ability of the mediator to get the other party to move on a frozen issue.

Looking for Movement

The main concern of the mediator in determining what is to be the first issue in the mediation is to find a subject that will be conducive to bringing the parties together. If he selects such a subject, the parties will realize that movement is possible, that compromise is not the evil they had feared, and that further discussion may generate further movement on both sides. Beginnings are the hardest, but when movement is generated there may be sufficient accommodation to produce a real momentum toward settlement. The turning point in the mediation comes when the teams both recognize that it is not a question of "winning" or "losing" but rather of finding compromises that are acceptable to both parties.

Mediator's Power to Change Issues

Gaining such recognition may be the mediator's objective, and it may be achieved if the correct choice of initial issues is made. But the selection of the wrong issue, or extreme rigidity on the first issue by one or both of the parties may frustrate the process. If that occurs, the mediator must try another tack. The mediator is in the unique position of being able to change subjects or issues with relatively little accountability. A team cannot know whether a change of subject was initiated by the mediator or by the other team, or indeed whether a seemingly new subject is in fact related to the subject that was initially under discussion.

So if the first issue does not fly, the mediator can readily shift gears to begin discussion of another issue. "By the way, on another subject, is there any room for movement on this other issue?" "Do you think you could adjust your position in this respect, maybe making it more palatable to the other team?"

Pushing and prodding by the mediator may uncover a subject on which there is a willingness to change positions and begin moving toward settlement. Even if there is no change of position by both parties on the same issue, the mediator is in the position to begin to combine issues, or put together packages that will encourage movement in one area to induce movement by the other side in another area.

Summary

Inducing the parties to focus on a single issue at the outset of the mediation may be extremely difficult. Each party has a number of proposals; each is wary of the proposals made by the other side. Above all, each is fearful that any backing away from the proposals it has been supporting so rigidly will be viewed as a sign of willingness to make concessions all the way to Waterloo.

The stakes in this matter are perceived by the teams to be high. For the mediator, however, the selection of the first issue is more an annoyance than a serious impediment. The mediator recognizes that all items have to be dealt with at one time or another, and that there will be no settlement unless both teams agree to each of its elements.

Nevertheless the tactical sparring must proceed. When it is brought to an end by the team's or the mediator's efforts, the mediation will shift into a higher gear.

9

INTERIM SESSIONS WITH ONE TEAM

After the initial meeting with each of the teams, what does the mediator do next? Each team has argued the merits and urgency of its position. Each team has excoriated the other, citing its adversary's intransigence as the sole reason for impasse. Each team has, in most cases, urged the mediator to get the other team to move, stating a willingness to reexamine its own position in return. Each side clearly sees the impasse as the other side's fault.

The mediator, now out in the hall, has two choices: return to the first team or try to work with the spokespersons.

If the meeting with the employer was successful in producing an adjustment in its position, a return to the union team would be worthwhile at this point, so that the mediator can report the employer's new position. The same might be true if the employer adhered to its position but asked for a clarification of the union stance. Even if the two initial meetings produced no change in position, the mediator might opt to return to the union team if only to report the lack of progress and urge a change in some element of the team's stand in order to start the ball rolling.

The mediator may decide instead to meet with one or both spokespersons, particularly if the initial sessions with each produced no change in position. If the mediator has had prior dealings and a trusting relationship with one of the leaders, he might call that person out into the hall for a suggestion on how to proceed. The mediator who felt sufficiently comfortable with both leaders and knew that they got along might call both out for a skull session on what to do next.

This chapter covers the mediator's role with the respective teams. The next chapter covers the mediator's role with the spokespersons.

Reporting to the Team

Whether it be during the meeting just after the initial session with each team, or after a series of relays between the team caucus rooms, the mediator starts the session with a report on the status of the mediation.

The team, after all, has been alone and out of range of the "action" for as long as the mediator has been out of sight. It has no sense of whether the mediator made any inroads upon the "rigidity" of the other team. Whatever message was relayed through the mediator—a request for clarification or a suggested bit of movement on a particular point or two—team members have no idea what has happened. They have been waiting, and probably feel they have waited too long. The teams tend to be insensitive to the length of time they spend in preparing their proposals; they are engrossed and don't watch the hours tick by. Despite the time they themselves take, they seldom understand that the other side also needs time to consider and respond to them. The mediators should try to prevent excessively long waiting periods for the teams, perhaps by coming back into the room every few minutes to report that the other team is still meeting, or by giving the team some task to perform as they leave to go to the other side. My favorite technique is to ask the team to make a calculation of the cost of some of the economic items that are bound to come up later. I also suggest that they should devote the time by themselves to working out a "fall-back" position, even though it may not be needed, in order to expedite the process.

When the mediator returns to a team's caucus, team members are pleased to again become the focus of action and eager to learn the results of the mediator's excursion into enemy territory. The mediator reports the other side's latest position, which probably is not as favorable as the team had hoped for. It is usually but an interim step in the ongoing jockeying of both parties. The report is important not only because of its content, but also because it provides the mediator with a critical opportunity to assess the reaction of the group when little progress has been made. Will the report be met with alarm, resentment, a shrug, a smile? The reaction of the individual team members to the report is of great importance to the mediator and may convey much more than the spokespersons words of acknowledgement. It may indicate to the mediator whether or not the effort is on the right track. It may demonstrate whether the gap remains wide or whether the teams are close to settlement. Or the message may be that the potential for progress is there provided a palatable response can be coaxed out of the team by the mediator. Accordingly, the report should be presented factually and in a businesslike manner, and with as little personal emotional involvement as possible.

Many times the report the mediator relays is a simple one, such as: "Tell them we will agree to their proposal but only if it is for two uniforms apiece instead of three." Or, "We won't agree to any uniforms but will provide a $100 credit at Jones Uniform Store for each employee."

My practice on receiving and verifying a message from the other team is to "clear it" first with the leader of the waiting team. I do this by poking my head into the caucus room and asking the spokesperson to come out a moment. I then recite the message as written and announce that I'm going to read it to the team. The spokesperson appreciates the extra attention, and it may help to avoid a donnybrook. The leader may say, "The team will hit the roof, I'd better go prepare them." Or, "Don't read it first—prepare them by telling them how difficult it was to get any movement." Sometimes the leader's negative reaction may prompt the mediator to return to the other team without ever reporting the message. The leader, for example, may say something like, "Wait a minute. They offered a $200 credit in direct negotiations on the same proposal—you'd better remind them of that. It may just be an oversight." In some particularly tense mediations the spokesperson has said to me, "If you bring that in to the team, they'll just get up and leave and there will be a strike. Take it back and say that as spokesperson I am rejecting it. If they insist on your reporting it to the team, do so, but remember, I warned you."

After the discussion with the spokesperson, the mediator, unless sent back to the other team, reports the message as given, preferably reading an exact quote that he has previously secured from, and verified by reading it back to, the other team.

It should be noted that the relaying of messages from team to team is not the universal practice of all mediators. Most will do it on some occasions. But there is a sizeable group of mediators who reject the notion that it is the mediator's function to relay proposal and counter-proposal. These mediators believe that the mediator is integrally tied to the negotiating process and should do no more than clear away the impediments to repeated joint meetings. According to this view, the mediator should perhaps move between teams to secure clarifications or resolve problems about what issue is on the table, or when joint sessions should be held; but they should refrain from actually carrying changes in positions, or responses, or alterations of proposals. Responsibility for announcing moves should remain within the teams, and there should be direct communication, across the bargaining table.

Although, as noted earlier, this procedure takes additional time arranging for the groups to meet and to separate, and does risk more direct confrontation, it has its strengths. It permits direct observation of reactions to proposals. The team itself sees how a proposal is received instead of having it relayed, either accurately or in muted terms, by a third party. For the team to witness the other side's reaction to a proposal—its outrage or its passivity, team dissension or team unity—is far more effective than receipt only of the perception of the mediator.

Additionally, direct presentation avoids the possibility of error on the part of the mediator. If the spokesperson errs in a direct presentation, it is the team's responsibility and not that of the mediator.

Unattributed Proposals

Despite the benefits of direct confrontation, there are a multitude of situations in which both teams may believe that it is better for the mediator to relay a response than for the team to do it. For instance, the mediator may be requested to transmit the information that a team lacks the authority to make an affirmative response, or that the team does not wish to be seen as being a party to a developing compromise. Certainly there are many instances where the message is clear—"Tell them yes," or "Our position is . . . " But there are also many times when a team is unwilling to state a position directly. Its reluctance may stem from fear that its stand on related issues may be compromised or other portions of its proposal may be jeopardized. A money proposal is an excellent example. For the management team to propose a $500 increase in a benefit in order to reach agreement on that issue may be interpreted by the union team as meaning that the $500 is on the table, or in its pocket, and that intransigence may bring a further sweetening of the pot.

In such cases the mediator may be a useful conduit for a proposal that is not attributed to the team and not binding upon it. Take the case of the employer willing to provide $500 more in benefits to wrap up one of the issues in dispute. It might tell the mediator that it is willing to provide the additional dollar amount but does not want to open the door to union efforts to obtain more. The mediator might then offer to sound the union out without committing the employer. With the $500 offer "in his pocket," the mediator could report to the union team not that the employer has made the offer but rather that "I have a suggestion for wrapping up that item. Would a somewhat higher dollar amount induce you to close it out?" or "What if I could get $500 more? Would that take care of that issue?" The mediator is not making a firm "proposal" but is presenting what one mediator calls a "supposal" and another calls a "what if." The mediator must be careful not to label it as an offer; he must not say that the employer proposed it, or perhaps even that the employer is aware of it. The union may *suspect* the employer has authorized the proposal, and a sophisticated union representative would realize that the mediator would not suggest a basis for settlement unless he already knew that it was acceptable to the other party. But the vagueness in authorization provides valuable insulation for the employer that would not be available if the proposal were made directly across the bargaining table. If the mediator makes the "supposal" to the union, neither the union nor its representative can go after the employer for having put the $500 on the table. The true maker of the proposal is anonymous. Even if asked, the mediator can decline to identify the sponsor: "I'm making the proposal," or "I didn't say that the employer is making it," or perhaps even, tongue in cheek, "It depends on whether it's acceptable."

The mediator may sometimes be caught in a cross fire of what ifs, with the union saying, for example, "We won't agree to that, but if you can go a little higher you have a deal. We can't commit ourselves yet to taking the issue off the table, or to dropping our $800 demand, but if you revise the proposal you just made upward to $550, that would do it."

The mediator must then return to the employer with the $550 counterproposal, without acknowledgement of the union's initiation of it. "Would you raise your figure to $550 for a settlement?" Or "If you make it $550, I think you'll have a deal. I can't guarantee it, but I think that would do it."

In all of these exchanges the mediator ostensibly is the one making the proposal, but each party has confidence in the mediator's reliability and experience and assumes a comparable degree of trust between the mediator and the other party. Both teams go along with the game because they know that, although it is a charade, it masks real bargaining between the mediator and one or both of the teams. If it is carried out smoothly enough, the party to whom a proposal is offered will never know for sure whether the ideas being floated emanate from the mediator or from the other side.

Assessing Progress and Stimulating Movement

Whether or not the mediator enters a team meeting with a specific proposal intended to bring about movement, at some point the team may ask for an assessment of the progress of the mediation. More likely, the mediator will initiate a discussion of progress to date, deploring the fact that so few issues have been resolved and hoping to stimulate more rapid movement.

Such an appraisal is helpful in alerting the team to the difficulties the mediator is experiencing. The mediator may relate the problems the other team is having with a particular issue, or may discuss the delays being caused by the teams' refusal to move further. The parties are in a sort of isolation for long periods of time during a mediation, interrupted only by occasional questions or proposals brought in by the mediator. They tend to lack perspective as to the overall shape of the mediation. Is real progress being made, or are only minor cosmetic moves being made while major positions remain static? Are the efforts of the mediator just so much wheel-spinning, or do they represent essential preliminaries to substantial movement later?

Opening New Issues

A frank discussion of the status of the mediation by the mediator may be helpful in steering the parties into more meaningful areas. If the team is told that there can be no settlement unless one of the recalcitrant parties makes a move, that warning may be enough to trigger a change of position on the more central issue or issues, if indeed settlement is desired. The team may reach this conclusion on its own from the pessimistic tenor of the mediator's report. The mediator may send the message to each team directly, and is in a unique position to steer the teams to the issue or issues the mediator deems ripe for exploration.

The sought-after change of position may come only after such prodding from the mediator. One of the most crucial contributions that can be made by the mediator is to raise doubts in the minds of team members as to the parties' current positions. When the team expresses a position of adamancy, it may help to stimulate movement if the mediator can point out the weaknesses in that position and the risks raised by adherence to it. If, for instance, the issue is the union team's refusal to agree to any subcontracting of work, the mediator might explain management's view that outsiders are needed to do certain work for which the facility lacks the necessary equipment, or emphasize the determination of the employer to take a strike on the issue unless a compromise can be reached. In conveying this information the mediator might emphasize the impact on the bargaining unit that might result if, for instance, the employer is not allowed to contract out the building of a new warehouse in which additional bargaining unit employees would be employed. The mediator might suggest changes in the union's position that might induce movement on the other side. Usually it is preferable to suggest a number of alternatives to avoid the impression conveyed by a single suggestion, i.e., that the suggestion is the only alternative and that the other team has authorized or requested the mediator to propose it on management's behalf.

To overcome the union's refusal to countenance any subcontracting whatsoever, the mediator might suggest language permitting limited subcontracting where the necessary skills or equipment are not available in the bargaining unit, for example, or only if no employees are on layoff, or not more than once per year, or only after discussion with the union. Not only does a variety of suggestions give the team a number of possibilities to choose from; it also permits the mediator to assess the reactions to the several suggestions and thus determine what sort of compromise on the issue may prove acceptable at a later stage of the mediation.

Pet Issues

In some cases the greatest impediment to progress is the risk of being sidetracked by a pet project of a team leader. Insistence on negotiating about the right to wear fraternal emblems on uniform shirts not only may take too much time, but may also cause frustration and increase rigidity on other, more important items for both teams. One of the mediator's functions is to suggest the elimination or at least the tabling of such impediments to meaningful negotiations. The mediator can accomplish this by suggesting that the issue is producing hostility that might have an adverse effect on the rest of the proposer's package and that maybe it would be better to change subjects to let the teams cool off for a while. The issue, it should be emphasized, will come up again later and must be resolved at some point if there is to be a settlement.

Mediator's Prior Experience

The mediator can also help by giving the team the benefit of his experience in other negotiations and his knowledge of prevailing practice elsewhere, thereby encouraging a more realistic assessment by the team of its proposal or position. Frequently such comments as "Your proposal would be a first for this state," or "You're the only jurisdiction in the metropolitan area that *doesn't* have that provision," will be enough to stimulate rethinking of a position to bring it closer to conformity with prevailing practice in other jurisdictions.

Ratification Requirements

The mediator sometimes may be able to stimulate a change in position by pointing out that the final agreement must be ratified, particularly if the proposal in question is one that has appeal to the ratifying group. Incorporating that proposal might increase the chances for approval of an agreement that otherwise might not be ratified. Since the negotiation process is, after all, a political process, such sensitivity to the needs or demands of the rank and file or of the management group, even if on a trivial matter, might be crucial to achieving a settlement.

Dealing With Multiple Issues

Sometimes the large number of outstanding issues may itself be an impediment to movement. If one of the parties—presumably the union—is insisting on concessions in many areas, the other party may be unwilling to grant any of the demands until it has some assurances that its opposite number is serious about settling and not merely positioning itself for fact finding. The absence of an offer on any of the demands may be due to a fear that concessions will be expected on all items, making movement on any one risky.

In such a case the mediator might seek to remedy the situation by suggesting that a proposal be made on one of the items, dependent on the dropping of the others. Alternatively, the mediator might suggest that the team with the extensive list of demands consider unilaterally dropping some of the items as a means of reducing the threat to the other side and inducing it to make a counterproposal.

Tackling Key Issues

A possible way for the mediator to stimulate further movement is to shift the discussion to the high-priority issues of both teams. "What do you think their greatest need is?" "Do you think you could grant it in exchange for their granting your greatest need?" Each party frequently fails to recognize that the other side has an equally intense commitment and that its needs are just as real. If sensitized to the other side's priorities by the mediator, a team may be willing to adjust its position on an issue it views as relatively minor that is, nevertheless, a matter of high priority to the other team. The other team might then be willing to make a concession in an area that is of importance to it. The content of the proposals will evolve by trial and error and exchange and response. What is important is the role of the mediator in making the stymied parties aware of an avenue of exploration they might otherwise have ignored—the two teams' respective priorities.

Warning of Consequences

Probably one of the most effective devices that can be utilized by a mediator to break a stalemate is, as noted earlier, the recitation of the "chamber of horrors," the listing of what can be expected to happen if the stalemate persists. Often the teams fail to recognize the consequences of their intransigence. They assume the other side will eventually give in. One way of demonstrating to a team what it is risking by its rigidity is to walk it through the consequences of not altering its position.

Usually both negotiating teams have thoughtful and responsive members. Although they may be committed to the team and its objectives, they are usually pragmatic enough to listen to reason and to weigh the need for settlement against their team loyalty. The message of the chamber of horrors usually gets through. It may not elicit an instant response, but it is received and will usually result in a position change eventually.

There are, to be sure, teams that are so committed, so suicidal, that any warnings or suggestions from the mediator will be ignored. But the resulting chaos should not be on the mediator's conscience for want of trying. The mediator cannot and should not try to force a settlement. All he can do, or should do, when discussing a stalemate with a team is to pose some provocative questions the team might not have thought about or make suggestions that it may recognize as being in its self-interest to pursue.

If the mediator's questions or suggestions have the desired effect of getting the team to reexamine its position, it is important that the team be given time to do so. It would be wise for the mediator to withdraw for a few minutes, even before being asked to do so. An explanation that "I have to make a few phone calls, I'll be in my room," or "I want to check something with the other team, I'll be back in 10 minutes," may be effective in providing the team with the needed time for reconsidering its position.

Assessing the Team

One of the attributes that distinguishes the highly proficient mediator from the neophyte is the ability to discern reactions and attitudes from what is said and what is not said. The mediator must be able to apply that information to the situation at hand and determine what course of action and what terminology to use to encourage movement in the direction that appears to offer the best hope of settlement.

True, the mediator may have made such an assessment in the initial meetings of the teams, but positions change and attitudes change. The mediator must be alert to these changes in order to capitalize on them in the move toward settlement. Team members' reactions to proposals, their passing of notes, their silences, and their body language throughout a session may tell the mediator a good deal more about the team's mood than words could ever do. Words don't tell the whole story and may be contrary to the true sentiment of the team. A declaration of firmness by the spokesperson that was supported by nods of team members in the initial meeting may now be accompanied by smirks or furtive glances among team members or even a request for a caucus in the midst of the defense of a position.

If the mediator describes the chamber of horrors and is met with a flat statement that "We realize the consequences, we're holding to the demand," it sends a different message than a "We'll think about it," or "Let us caucus," or "If we move, will they?" The usual team discipline, which places the spokesperson in the position of making all presentations, may be a disadvantage in this situation. The mediator will benefit from and perhaps even encourage the views of individual team members, particularly if they differ from the leader's stance. If the spokesperson is an experienced professional, however, there is less need for the mediator to talk past the leader to the team. The leader may be presumed to have his internal team politics under control and will tell the mediator when he needs help.

The mediator must be cautious in drawing inferences from the conduct of the parties, for it is easy to misinterpret the alleged signals. Perhaps the greatest danger is that of misrepresenting them in discussions with the other team. An erroneous conclusion that a change of position on an issue is impending, if reported to the other side, may cause that side to alter its position in reliance on the impression expressed by the mediator. The result may be a very red-faced mediator.

Maintaining Confidence in the Mediator

Although the mediator in the initial joint session warned both parties that he would be coming down hard on them in the team caucuses, it is not unusual for a team to conclude that the mediator is tilting too much toward the other side. Indeed, both teams may be distrustful at the same time. Many of the messages the mediator brings to each team, after all, are rejections of proposals and admonitions to change positions. And there is always the question of whether the mediator is telling all that he hears. Although earning the simultaneous distrust of both teams may testify to the mediator's impartiality, the mediator can survive only with the trust of both.

Enjoying both sides' confidence is important not because it feeds the mediator's ego or assures his designation in future cases. It is a question of the mediator's effectiveness in bringing the parties to a settlement in the case at hand. Each side must be convinced that the mediator is being even-handed. Each side must be confident that the mediator, if not on its side, is at least not prejudiced in the other side's favor.

In order to assure that the parties do regard the outsider as neutral, it is important that the mediator make a conscious though subtle effort to maintain the parties' confidence. One way is to avoid expressing personal views on the items in dispute. The effective mediator is able to muster numerous arguments pro and con on any issue that is under consideration. It adds very little to those arguments for the mediator to state a personal belief on the merits of a proposal unless he is asked to do so by both teams. Such a declaration, if negative, will be thought to have been instigated by or offered on behalf of the other team. An affirmative opinion, on the other hand, will quickly find its way back to the other side and create similar suspicion of bias. Mediators should abide by the adage "Don't express your personal view to either side unless you want both teams to know it."

The mediator also must avoid personal comments about the members of either team, whether positive or negative. Personal views, particularly if critical, will get back to the other team even faster than opinions on substance. If a team is aware that the mediator never criticizes anyone on the other side, it should realize that there is likewise no denigrating of its members in the other team's caucuses.

A third way to build confidence is to keep the teams regularly informed as to what is going on. Isolation is bound to breed suspicion, each team assuming that if the mediator isn't spending time with it he must be more comfortable with the other group. Even if the circumstances of the case and the attitudes of the teams prohibit an equal allocation of time to the two groups, the mediator should try to compensate for any neglect of one team by making periodic reports to it of what has been happening.

Sometimes the establishment of confidence and trust requires doing things that would be unnecessary if the mediator's neutrality were unquestioned. The mediator may be asked to take a proposal to the other team even though it is sure to be rejected or has in fact been rejected in a prior caucus with that team. Agreeing to a request to carry out even a pointless venture may be an effective way to establish credentials in the eyes of a doubting or suspicious team.

Socializing at Breaks

The public perception of the mediator is of one who works with single-mindedness toward settlement, a person who is all business. Even though the mediator may joke or engage in banter from time to time with one or both teams, it may be thought that his lightheartedness is a calculated attitude adopted to create an atmosphere conducive to settlement. It is therefore helpful, for the mediator to be with one or both of the parties during some of breaks, or traveling to or from a session, when relationships tend to be more informal, more relaxed, and less threatening.

The structure of the mediation process usually confines the teams to separate rooms, often for extended periods, giving them time to conjure up all sorts of misimpressions of the other side through the intimidating proposals and rejections that are passed to them by the mediator. The joint sessions that are held from time to time are likely to be all business. Even though the members of the two teams work and socialize with one another throughout the rest of the year, they are forced into isolated camps throughout the mediation.

There are certain things the mediator can do to compensate for these periods of separation and to instill an element of informality that might help to humanize the process as well as the teams' perceptions of the mediator. One is the sharing of coffee breaks. One or both teams are likely to have coffee and refreshments on hand during the mediation, particularly for all-night sessions. There have been times when, feeling that some socializing would help the relationship, I have told the parties I was going out to get some coffee and doughnuts for a team that did not bring anything. The party with the ample supply has, on more than one occasion, said, "We have plenty; have them come in and get their coffee here." Even if such an invitation is not forthcoming, the mediator may be able to get the parties together by saying, "I am getting enough coffee for both teams. Let's get together for a break."

Meal breaks offer another opportunity for socializing between the teams. The mediation usually upsets normal meal period habits, with each party busy in caucus or awaiting the response of the other team. Timing is frequently of the essence, and the teams are reluctant to leave the scene for fear that an opportunity for movement might be lost. Because of the continuous nature of the mediation, it is really up to the mediator to declare a meal break for the teams if there is to be one. Otherwise, the teams either have food brought in, or each takes separate breaks at times that the mediator agrees will not disrupt the process. A common occasion is when a team has just given a complex proposal to the other team for its consideration.

Sometimes the mediator can capitalize on the situation. For example, in a recent mediation the author was meeting with the management team when one of them said, "We were just going to order some Chinese food for our team. Will you join us?" I suggested that maybe it would be nice for both groups to eat together, adding, "I'll go see what they want." "Well, we thought we'd just eat by ourselves," was the response, to which I commented, "That's what they said you'd say. Why not invite them and surprise them. Maybe it will soften their attitude toward you, and their positions." The employer agreed to a joint dinner and, after some prodding, even agreed to pay for everyone's meal. I took the menu to the union team, got their order, the food was sent for, and the union team was called in when it arrived. Everyone seemed to enjoy the joint meal, everyone chatted amicably, and I even noted a few private head-to-head conferences around the room with people from the two teams. I am not sure the joint meal provided a great leap forward to settlement, but I am sure that it provided a welcome respite from the polarity that typifies most mediations.

Trying Out New Packages

Throughout the numerous team meetings that occur in the mediation, the mediator is usually coming in with a response or a proposal and then taking the reply to the other side. There comes a time when that process hits a snag or the mediator feels it is taking more time than the results justify. The latter is particularly likely to be the case if the mediator has a deadline for departure, or if the parties are unwilling to confront the fact that *they* have a deadline.

In such circumstances the mediator might decide that it is worthwhile to try a new approach. One suggestion is a trade-off of items that the parties have been dealing with independently. Alternatively, the mediator might suggest a change in focus with attention turning to new, more crucial items than the parties were dealing with in their preceding exchanges. Or the mediator might suggest a package deal combining a number of items that he believes will appeal to both parties. Whether the package will be composed of minor issues or of high priority issues may depend on what subjects the parties have been discussing and on the time sequence. After a number of hours dealing with individual small items, it may seem worthwhile to deal with these items as a group. On the other hand, the mediator might decide the time is ripe to switch the parties' focus to the larger, more controversial items that are at the heart of their dispute.

The parties themselves may recognize that they are deadlocked and that a new approach is needed, but not be able to drop proposals or indicate that trade-offs are possible. One team may suggest that the mediator be the one to formulate a new proposal. Sometimes the parties unwittingly do some of the packaging on their own, often by omission. Expanded funeral leave may figure prominently for a time in a union proposal on paid leaves of absence, always being rejected by the employer. Then at some point funeral leave disappears from the proposal. Some mediators might ask, "Are you dropping funeral leave?"

Others would say: "Now let me read you back what I have as your total leave proposal...." The latter approach is risky since there is always a chance that the item was accidently omitted. It is better for the mediator to make certain that he is relaying the true package, perhaps by reading the proposal and then adding, "You realize there is no mention of funeral leave," and go on to something else. The spokesperson may not want to state the withdrawal specifically, and may respond to the mediator's question by saying, "The proposal as you read it is our total proposal on leaves." Verification could also be accomplished by calling the leader out into the hall to point out the omission of the funeral leave.

How the package proposal is presented to the other side is a different matter. When meeting with the other team to announce the proposal, the mediator would simply read the proposal. Asked about funeral leave, the mediator could readily recount the exchanges with the other team and his conclusion that funeral leave had been dropped. Careful notes on those exchanges might protect the mediator if later the first team should deny having dropped the funeral leave proposal.

Package proposals are made as totalities, to be accepted or rejected as a whole. The receiving party ordinarily is not free to pick and choose the elements that it prefers. The mediator should make it clear when taking a proposal and relaying it to the other side that it is an all-or-nothing offer, that it is not possible to take some elements and reject others. In a package that provides a 6-percent salary increase but no improvement in health insurance, for example, the union team cannot say, "We will take the 6 percent. We agree to that, but we still want to negotiate on health insurance."

The requirement of acceptance or rejection of the entire package does not preclude the receiving team from making a counter offer rearranging the package: "We can't accept that package as offered but would settle for 6 percent on salary and 1 percent more in health insurance." There may appear to be no difference between the responses but in the former there is an acceptance of part of the package while in the latter there is recognition that a portion of the package is acceptable but that both subjects are interdependent and still open for negotiation.

Bolstering the Spokesperson

The mediator may on occasion solicit input from team members to encourage expressions that differ from presentations of the team leader. Nonetheless, the mediator must recognize that the leader plays a crucial role in determining the success or failure of the mediation. The leader may suspect the mediator of trying to undercut his authority by talking directly to team members, even in the presence of the leader. Therefore, before leaving a team caucus the mediator must make clear to team members and the spokesperson that he recognizes and relies on the spokesperson. The effort necessary to bolster the standing of the spokesperson may be in direct proportion to the mediator's success in getting the team members to express alternative and perhaps contrary positions to those taken by the spokesperson.

The mediator must not allow his direct approaches to team members to rupture the team structure. The mediator acts appropriately in listening to the comments and reactions of team members as long as they are freely and voluntarily offered. But he should not go behind the spokesperson's back to solicit members' views, nor should he pursue direct dealings with team members when the spokesperson forecloses them.

Regardless of the extent or spontaneity of these direct exchanges, the mediator should thereafter reassert the commitment to deal with the leader as the established channel of communication with the team. This can be done at the end of the session with the team by summarizing the instructions given to the mediator and verifying that any new offers are authorized by the spokesperson. It can also be done by asking the leader for an opinion as to the strategy to be followed next. This is particularly welcome to the spokesperson if he is treated by the mediator as an "expert" or a "pro" in the presence of the whole team. The mediator can assure the leader that "Any off-the-record discussions we may have had as individuals in this session are for my ears only. I'll continue to report to the other team on the basis of what Jim, as spokesperson, authorizes me to do."

Beyond such statements in the presence of the team, the mediator can offer private reassurances to the spokesperson. But probably the most potent reassurance comes after the session when the mediator returns to the room, asks the leader to step out into the hall for an exchange, and shows by deed that he is communicating with the team through the leader. That is the subject of the next chapter.

Summary

The mediator's meetings with the individual teams are an essential element in advancing the mediation. They reassure the team members of their involvement and importance in the process. They provide an occasion for measuring progress or lack of progress by talking over the issues and attitudes of both teams with the mediator. They give the mediator an opportunity to assess the determination and attitudes of team members on the issues. And they enable the mediator to encourage the reexamination of rigid positions, to explore new approaches, and to reassure the team and the spokesperson that the process is working.

10
CAUCUSES WITH SPOKESPERSONS

The conventional expectation is that the mediator will spend most of the time in mediation moving from one team to the other relaying messages, leaving the room after delivering a message to permit the team to caucus. There are many times when such a shuttling procedure is the standard for the entire mediation, particularly if a team insists that all team members must attend all discussions with the mediator. It may be the exclusive way of maintaining contact with a team in such cases.

The Spokespersons

The teams do have designated spokespersons whose role it is to speak for the team in direct negotiations with the other side. That is one of the established ground rules of negotiations. Generally that role is continued in mediation, the spokesperson being recognized as the team's representative in sessions with the mediator. The spokesperson may also control the team caucuses. The fact that an individual is the spokesperson for the team, however, does not necessarily mean that person controls the team. The power within the team may be divided, with the role of the spokesperson being limited to that of chairperson of internal discussions. The power and authority may rest in another person, making the spokesperson little more than an observer in the discussions and a mouthpiece for external contacts, expressing positions, assents, rejections, and modifications of the team's position only after discussion with the team, or instructions from whoever in fact controls the team.

There are two main types of spokespersons. They may be in-house, full-time employees of the establishment or the party they represent. Or they may be outside consultants brought in from state or national organizations to which the parties belong, such as an employer's federation or a national union, or may be hired as ad hoc professionals, such as consultants or attorneys, hired on a case-by-case basis.

In-House Spokesperson

Spokespersons may be shrewd and experienced negotiators, independent within their organization and, even if without authority on substantive matters, respected for their expertise in the procedures of negotiation and mediation. Spokespersons of this caliber are every bit as good as outside professionals. More likely, particularly in new or immature collective bargaining relationships, the team spokesperson is an amateur in labor relations whose principal position is that of, say, personnel director, superintendent, department supervisor, chief shop steward, or local union president. Frequently the occupant holds the position for only one or, at most, a few years, depriving the team of continuity of experience in negotiations. Such a spokesperson may be new to negotiations and inexperienced in the subtleties of the process. He or she may also be unsure of the rights and responsibilities of the position and furthermore may be incapable of providing effective guidance to the team in the formulation, adjustment, or timing of positions in negotiations or mediation. The pressures from various team members in support of their pet proposals may be so strong that the in-house spokesperson who has to work with the team members on a daily basis throughout the year is unwilling or unable to override it. The difficulty of saying no to such confreres may in fact have contributed to the lack of prior success in direct negotiations and the need to turn to mediation. The spokesperson may know of the skeletons in team members' closets, but the team members may have similar knowledge about their spokesperson and thus be able to restrict the spokesperson's independence.

Additionally, the in-house spokesperson may have a strong personal stake in some of the critical proposals and be incapable of taking a detached view. A police-officer spokesperson ready to retire may have so great a personal interest in a severance or pension proposal that he won't budge from it. A personnel officer on the management side, for that matter, may stand to benefit from such a proposal and be less than forceful in opposing it. Management team awareness of sympathy toward a union proposal on the part of its spokesperson may lead to tension within the team and mistrust of the spokesperson.

Professional Spokesperson

If the parties are sufficiently sophisticated to secure a professional spokesperson, many of the problems associated with in-house amateurs are avoided. The outside professional is more likely to be looked to as the procedural expert on how best to achieve the team's objectives. With outside hiring and a dollar commitment also comes increased respect. The outside professional still has the problems of coping with the various team constituencies and dealing with the power source as to negotiating strategy and tactics. The outsider can more effectively spell out the consequences of not settling. There is less likelihood of mistrust of personal motives. The outsider usually has the required experience in handling internal as well as external pressures in the negotiations. Such an expert is, in fact, a mediator between the outside world and the team.

The competence and independence of the spokespersons, as well as the confidence placed in them by their teams, will be tested in caucuses with the mediator.

Benefits of Spokesperson Caucuses

If the mediator is so fortunate as to have spokespersons who are able to extricate themselves from the constant surveillance of their teams, not only the mediator but the teams may benefit. The effective utilization of spokespersons depends in large measure on the compatibility of their personalities and settlement goals with those of the mediator, their authority to engage in such collateral and often off-the-record discussions, and their security with their teams. The mediator may be able to utilize the spokespersons to accelerate the process and to prevent false starts and tactical errors. Much depends on the perspective and authority of the spokespersons, but the mediator would seek to work through the spokespersons away from their respective teams only if convinced that this would not harm the spokespersons' standing with their teams and that they shared with the mediator the goal of securing a rapid and mutually acceptable settlement of the dispute.

Insights Into Team Thinking

If the spokespersons are sufficiently secure in their positions with their teams, they can provide valuable insights to the mediator as to the atmosphere within the team and its views as to the progress of the mediation. They can tell the mediator if team members feel there has been too much pushing or are getting suspicious of the mediator's neutrality or, on the other hand, if the team feels that the mediator has not pushed hard enough. A spokesperson can advise the mediator as to the priorities of the team, and its willingness to compromise on certain issues. There may be perspectives the mediator might not have gained by direct talks with the team members themselves, and certainly attitudes the spokesperson could not have articulated in the presence of the team.

Assessing Positions

The spokesperson can also assist the mediator in assessing positions and proposals. If the mediator is about to bring a proposal to the team, either one of the mediator's own or a message from the other team, it is frequently useful to have a sounding board on which to try out the proposal prior to its announcement. A quick caucus with the spokesperson will alert the mediator to problems the proposal may create, or perhaps an insight as to the person to whom the proposal should be directed. It might also reveal the manner in which it should be made or phrased, or whether it is the right time to make the proposal. The spokesperson knows far better than the mediator whether a particular proposal at a particular time will work or will backfire. It is a great boon to the mediator to be able to have an ally in the spokesperson, particularly if there is trust between them and if the spokesperson is equally committed to settlement. Although an advocate, the helpful spokesperson should also have sufficient objectivity and sensitivity to the weaknesses and needs of the team to permit the mediator to present the best possible case in making proposals, or in seeking responses and moves from the team.

The Mediator's Mediator

In a sense, the willing spokesperson is the active ally of the mediator and becomes the mediator's mediator, serving as the go-between for the mediator with the team, suggesting how and when new offers should be made, preparing the ground for and helping to sell proposals, and urging cooperation with the mediator. Once the team is comfortable with that sort of relationship, it becomes a simple matter and indeed routine for the mediator to motion the spokesperson out into the hall to "try on for size" an offer or proposal from the other side, or to ask how something will be received, or to gain an off-the-record assessment of how the team feels on a particular issue. The spokesperson is also the beneficiary of such a frank relationship, for, after having established trust and confidence, the mediator is more likely to inform the spokesperson as to progress and concerns within the other team.

The mediator will, of course, cultivate such informal relationships with the spokespersons from both teams. In some relationships the spokespersons are not compatible or do not trust each other. But in a surprising (and from the mediator's point of view) comforting number of cases, particularly where they are outside consultants or attorneys, the spokespersons are sufficiently secure to permit joint caucuses together with the mediator. In many situations the relationship between the spokespersons is sufficiently cordial that the mediator is in the enviable position of being able to accomplish a great deal with the spokespersons alone, without the need for frequent forays into the dens of the respective teams. Experienced spokespersons are able to separate the "on-the-record" from the "off-the-record," provide accurate assessments as to what will fly and what will fail, and make moves without constantly checking back with their respective teams.

In such an atmosphere, where the spokespersons have advance authorization from their teams and are knowledgeable about the limits of their authority, it is possible for much of the mediation to turn into trilateral negotiations in the hall or mediator's room. For the mediator who is regularly consulted in a relationship, mediating contract after contract, such tripartite sessions become the norm of the mediation. The mediator will have direct contact with the teams only when there is an issue that the spokespersons believe the mediator should communicate directly or when a team requires a period of direct access to the mediator for the purpose of voicing its concerns.

Agreement in Caucus

In mature relationships where the mediation process is conducted in this fashion, it is not unusual for the two spokespersons and the mediator to do much of the negotiating in such caucuses, perhaps to the extent of working out the final agreement or its basic outline. This might occur even prior to the mediation during one of the preliminary sessions. Then, when the spokespersons and the mediator are in agreement as to the final package, they will jointly determine how best to overcome possible political problems and to "sell" the agreed-upon settlement terms to the respective teams.

The teams retain final authority and responsibility for the agreement, and the informal, off-the-record efforts of the two spokespersons bind neither themselves nor their teams. Yet it certainly simplifies and expedites the mediation effort to be able to cut through so much of the dross surrounding the real issues and focus on the priority items. The spokespersons and mediator can then work with the respective teams to make sure the proposed settlement is acceptable to them. Usually the teams accept their spokesperson's assurance that what had been worked out is in fact the best attainable settlement.

In cases where I have used this approach there have been situations where the anticipated settlement did not materialize. But the reason was that the package was wrong, not that the teams objected to their spokespersons' participation in the informal exchanges. It is indeed a luxury for the mediator to be able to meet together with two settlement-oriented advocates in a frank exchange as to what is attainable and acceptable and what is not, without having to commute between caucuses and repeat proposal after proposal, not knowing whether the offerings are reaching a receptive audience or what is needed to achieve a settlement.

Keeping the Team Involved

There are those who object to mediator-spokesperson caucuses on the ground that they deprive the teams of the opportunity to participate fully in the mediation and are an abuse of the mediator's authority. The mediator, in this view, makes himself a party to a clandestine effort on the part of the two spokespersons to "cut a deal." Unquestionably such an approach departs from the conventional notion of what a mediator is supposed to do, trudging back and forth between the two teams with proposals and counter offers.

In the author's view, however, mediation is merely a continuation of the negotiation process. Therefore it is no more objectionable to create a forum for the two designated spokespersons to meet voluntarily to work out a settlement than it is to have the two teams meet in the same room to accomplish the same thing—with more histrionics and polemics and delay. Providing an arena for the two spokespersons furthers the negotiation process. Certainly the detractors of this approach would have little difficulty with the two spokespersons agreeing to meet alone during the direct negotiations preceding mediation. Would they think it inappropriate for a mediator to assist the two in such discussions? In effect that is all the caucuses entail. The spokespersons presumably are authorized by their teams to engage in such an exchange or have the power to do so of their own volition. The mediator's role is merely to provide the forum and the assistance of a facilitator in such face-to-face talks.

Dangers of Spokesperson Caucuses

Despite my obvious preference for spokesperson caucuses as the most effective means for more rapid movement toward settlement, there are hazards in thus utilizing the spokespersons.

As noted earlier, the single most important factor in the success of the caucus is the security and independence of the spokesperson. The spokesperson may be weak and a mere front or mouthpiece for a power source within the team. Or there may be suspicion that the spokesperson will cut a deal for personal benefit, leaving the team with less than it thinks it is entitled to. It is often true, too, that the spokesperson may not feel sufficiently secure about the issues or the team, particularly if he is new to the process and lacks the confidence to go it alone without having the team present. The mediator may be enjoined from calling a spokesperson out into the hall, away from the rest of the team—either by his team, suspicious of the mediator or the spokesperson, or by the spokesperson himself, fearful of losing a power base or of being too closely identified with the mediator.

The team may suspect that the spokesperson is being brought under the influence of the mediator in "off the record" discussions, and fear that the spokesperson will prejudice its position by making hasty or unauthorized moves. If this is the case, the spokesperson may decline to participate in private meetings with the mediator, or at least avoid certain subjects in such discussions. The spokesperson may then be unwilling to hold serious and frank discussions with the mediator. He or she may indeed be the most militant member of the team—even more so than in the team meetings.

Much depends on the professionalism of the spokespersons. If they are regular employees of the enterprise, on either the bargaining unit side or the management side, they may be too closely associated with the issues and the politics of the relationship to be willing or able to provide a detached view of the proceedings. In addition, as active warriors, their goal may be victory and achievement of all demands rather than settlement and compromise of the demands.

But if they are removed from the daily fray and the personalization of the demands, they may prove to be more helpful to the mediator in caucus than in mediator–team meetings. The classic example of the semi-detached spokesperson is the state or international union representative or union attorney who is called in to represent the union in the mediation, or the representative of the state employers' federation or management attorney on the other side. Although such outsiders might have a stake in some of the issues, especially where the union is pressing for new benefits or the management association has determined to hold the line on certain items, they generally are more interested in settlement than the team members may be. At least they may have a more objective assessment of the attainable. They are, after all, usually away from home, are not particularly close to the individual team members, have a sense of detachment on the issues, and are aware of the prevailing rates and conditions and benefits achieved in agreements in comparable jurisdictions. In addition, they seek to make sure that the settlement in this jurisdiction is not out of line with those elsewhere, and that it does not establish any dangerous patterns.

The mediator may hope that such an individual has sufficient insight and independence and motivation toward settlement to be an ally in the effort to resolve the dispute. Obviously this hope may not be realized. The outside spokesperson may not have a goal of rapid settlement, but may fear that the procedure will end too soon, depriving him of income, or may be a militant determined to prevail without compromise or insensitive to the consequences of not settling in mediation. There may be greater interest in maintaining a state or national standard, or in achieving breakthrough, for its impact on later negotiations in other districts than in resolving the present dispute. Moreover, the spokesperson may not have a sufficiently secure relationship with the team to permit any wandering from the reservation; there may be a lack of trust on the part of the team, or a lack of experience with mediation or with the spokesperson. If the relationship is so fragile, time spent alone with the mediator may engender suspicion and mistrust and undercut whatever authority the spokesperson had. It might actually set the mediation back.

In such cases, mediator–spokesperson caucuses are to be avoided. The mediator should seek to protect the spokesperson's base and increase the trust between the spokesperson and the team. It may help to call a meeting with the team so that the spokesperson can explain the status of the caucus.

The mediator must be sensitive to the spokesperson's position and not expect him to stick his neck out for the mediator's convenience at the expense of his loyalty to his team. Forcing a spokesperson into a caucus with the mediator may cause the spokesperson to be accused of cutting a deal with the spokesperson for the other side for personal benefit.

In one state where the same spokespersons represented management and union sides in each of several mediations, we were compelled to eliminate hall caucuses because team members in a number of the towns believed we had a routine for resolving the disputes. They thought we had agreed that victories would be alternated as we proceeded from one mediation to the next.

There have been occasions when a high-minded, settlement-oriented spokesperson has spent considerable time fashioning what is unquestionably a reasonable settlement in caucus with the mediator and with the other spokesperson, only to have the settlement rejected by the team. If the spokesperson has not kept the team informed of changes in position, a settlement that bears little resemblance to the opening demands is bound to face rejection. The mediator may be reluctant to discourage such a process during a caucus, but it may be necessary to protect the spokesperson from going *too far* without the blessing or awareness of the team. The mediator, the spokesperson, and the two teams may in fact be set back by too rapid movement in the absence of participation or awareness on the part of the team.

Timing and Frequency of Caucuses

The mediator who is new to the relationship may find it difficult to tell whether the spokesperson or the team is comfortable with the mediator calling the spokesperson out into the hall for a discussion. It may be preferable in such a situation to begin the mediation with a series of meetings with the teams. This at least provides an opportunity to determine whether the spokesperson has the independence or the competence to be helpful to the mediator in a private session.

When the mediator believes there would be benefit from the personal insights of the spokesperson, or at least believes an exploration of the possibility of securing such insights would be desirable in a hall caucus, to ask the spokesperson to step out of the room for a moment is unlikely to be met with any objection. When the spokesperson is out in the hall, the question is asked, "What would your team say if I proposed X?" The spokesperson can decline to play, responding "Why don't you go in and try it?" But if, as is usually the case, the spokesperson does express an opinion without protest about being asked to do so away from the team, the mediator can feel free to use the device until told to desist by the person or until resistance is felt to that form of communication. It is, after all, for the spokespersons to decide whether they can afford to jeopardize their standing with their respective teams by taking part in such conversations, and whether it is in their and their teams' best interests that they do so. In my experience the spokespersons are more than likely to engage in such discussions, and are sufficiently alert to the interests of their teams and the need to maintain contact with them.

The mediator should not wait too long to try out the device. If the spokesperson is a willing player, a great deal of valuable one-on-one or tripartite time and opportunity for more rapid progress and valuable insight can be lost by adhering to the traditional go-between role.

The mediator may find it easier to engage in these caucuses than to commute between teams. It is important, however, not to permit convenience to outweigh the danger of the spokespersons' becoming suspect to their teams, or to jeopardize a potential settlement by permitting a team to be ignored for extended periods while the spokesperson is out of the room taking part in the more meaningful action. The teams are naturally suspicious of any deal cutting; even if they have authorized the participation in the caucuses, it must be remembered by spokespersons and mediator that the teams do retain the authority to approve or disapprove what is worked out. It would be regrettable if an otherwise acceptable solution were to be rejected because of a team's pique over not being kept informed of what was going on. Frequent reporting back during long-running caucuses may be needed if they are to continue until settlement is reached.

Maintaining the Spokesperson's Base

It might be wise for the mediator to meet with the respective teams from time to time during caucuses with the spokespersons to verify that the latter do indeed have the authority to participate in the caucuses or at least that their teams will tolerate their actions. The mediator must tactfully verify that a spokesperson is accurately relaying to the mediator and to the other spokesperson, if the caucus is joint, what is the true position of the team. Such confirmation can readily be secured by merely accompanying the spokesperson in a session to bring the team up to date about what has been discussed in the caucus. It is important when speaking to the team in caucus that the mediator not say more to the team than the spokesperson previously had relayed to the team.

Such visits to the team have two purposes. The first is to determine independently whether the spokesperson is reliable in assessing team support. Is the team supportive? Is it divided? Is the spokesperson accurately reporting back what is occurring? This checking, which must be done very carefully to avoid undercutting the spokesperson, is an essential assessment the mediator must make in every team meeting. If the views and opinions of team members appear to be divergent from those the spokesperson is presenting, the mediator might meet separately with the spokesperson to advise the latter of the mediator's perceptions in the session. Or the mediator might choose to avoid separate dealings with the spokesperson, concentrating instead on meetings with the entire team to make sure they are aware of all developments.

The second reason for closer communication with the team, particularly when dealing with an inexperienced spokesperson, is related to the preceding point. If the spokesperson is on a different wave length from the team, an alert team fully aware of all that is going on may be more likely to exert its influence on the spokesperson and to pressure the spokesperson to take positions that more accurately reflect the team's sentiment. The mediator must be careful not to undercut the spokesperson in such team meetings, but they may provide a vehicle for stimulating more cooperation and greater movement by the spokesperson. General comments about the need to reassess positions, to give up demands, and to find compromise positions are as applicable to spokespersons as to team members. The creation of doubts in the team members about the wisdom and achievability of what is currently on the table, coupled with "I've argued your position with them but they won't budge," may be sufficient to cause a reassessment and bring pressure to bear on the spokesperson to move more daringly toward new positions and potential compromise.

Summary

The practice of speaking to the spokesperson outside the reach of the team is a valuable option for the mediator. It permits a more accurate gauge of the correctness and acceptability of the mediator's moves and the progress toward settlement. To the extent that the spokespersons are willing to go beyond that to become active negotiators for their respective teams, the process of moving the parties toward settlement may well be facilitated.

On the other hand, the mediator must be aware that under some conditions caucuses with spokespersons can be counterproductive. If the mediator discovers that a spokesperson lacks authority or is failing to keep his team informed of all that is going on, it may be advisable to discontinue spokesperson caucuses in favor of meetings with the teams.

11
INTERIM JOINT SESSIONS
WITH BOTH TEAMS

If the mediator has lived up to the conventional expectation of relaying messages between the teams, with an occasional meeting of spokespersons in the hall, the result has been to keep the parties apart for a long while. Separate meetings with a team may tax the patience of that team, as well as the patience of the other team, which is waiting, unaware of what has happened to its last proposal. If this practice is utilized repeatedly in dealing with the teams over a period of hours or days, it may engender resentment with the process. Even if their direct negotiations were acrimonious at times, the teams at least were in direct communication and sight. They had the opportunity for informal discussions, off the record exchanges, and some humor. Above all, they had the chance to assess the reactions and interactions of the team members on the opposite side. With long intervals of separation during the mediation, the teams are deprived of the personal nuances that come from direct contact with the other side, and the perception of the absent team becomes one of rigidity and coldness.

Reestablishing Contact Between the Parties

It is essential for the mediator to bring the parties back to face-to-face contact in joint meetings on occasion, if only to restore an element of the human relationship between them. The occasions for such meetings might be meal breaks, or to provide an assessment of progress, or the resumption of the mediation after a break of days or weeks. Mediators who prefer that proposals be made by one team directly to the other across the table would automatically provide joint sessions whenever either side wished to announce a new position. Such mediators, accordingly, would not be confronted with this problem.

Most mediators, however, apparently comfortable with the efficiency of the shuttle approach, tend to overlook the need for joint sessions.

As a result, the calling of a joint session may arouse an expectation that something momentous will be announced, such as an agreement or, at the other extreme, termination of the mediation. To guard against this, the mediator should advise in his opening joint session that he plans to call the parties into joint session from time to time and should explain to each team just prior to each joint session why it is being called and what is expected to occur.

During joint sessions the mediator should seat himself at the head of the table and act with some formality and detachment to prevent either side from gaining the impression that the mediator feels closer to the other side. Ideally, the mediator will have been so successful in building trust and confidence that each side will assume the mediator would really prefer to be with it but "for appearances" must take the posture of a neutral.

Nonetheless, although the mediator may praise or castigate both parties in the joint sessions, it is important to avoid expressing any personal judgments on the substantive issues. For the mediator to voice pleasure, for instance, that one party finally agreed to the position adhered to so rigidly by the other party risks embarrassing the agreeing party for giving in while reinforcing the winning party's stubbornness. Indeed, the parties may both read messages of support into a mediator's expression of pleasure over an agreement on any issue brought before the joint session. The mediator must always avoid even the perception of siding with either party on any issue.

Why then the joint session? In addition to relieving the boredom that is bound to set in after extended periods of isolation from the other team, the joint sessions can help reinforce the credibility of the spokespersons' reports to their teams and can be capitalized upon by the mediator to further his goal of settlement in a number of other ways.

Reporting on Progress

The joint sessions provide an opportunity to confirm those subjects on which the parties have reached agreement. The purpose of such a description is not merely to congratulate the parties on their spirit of cooperation; more important, it is to verify those agreements the mediator reported as having been reached in the shuttles between the teams, and to make sure that both parties are fully aware of the terms of such agreements. While the mediator must steer clear of expressing a personal view as to whether the substance of any agreement is good or bad, it is essential to express an understanding as to the words that were agreed upon. Doing so in the presence of both parties assures that the messages relayed between the teams were accurate.

Disagreements as to what has been agreed to may occur even when the mediator is announcing the settlement terms. Whether the mediator was in error in concluding there was agreement, or one of the parties had second thoughts and reneged on a prior commitment, really matters little. The joint session in either case serves its purpose of verifying whether agreement on certain matters has in fact been reached. If not, then it is back to the separate team meetings for further discussions. If the mediator is sure there was agreement, he must insist that it be adhered to as an essential element of good faith bargaining, to prevent erosion of the mediator's credibility, and perhaps even as a necessary precondition to the mediator's continuing in a dispute settlement role.

Even if the parties confirm in the joint session what was earlier agreed to in caucus with the mediator, one or both still may deny that accord was ever reached on specific language and/or concepts. With the mediator's notes available as evidence of agreements reached in earlier separate sessions, however, reiteration of the agreement in the joint session usually serves as an effective deterrent to later disclaimers. Whether confirmation of agreement in joint session comes by vocal endorsement or by silent acquiescence, the mediator's pronouncement that "this is what you have agreed to" is usually sufficient to keep the agreement from coming unhinged.

Reporting Stalemate

Not all efforts at mediation are successful even on portions of an agreement, let alone on the agreement as a whole. Many times the most determined and conscientious efforts of the mediator bear no positive results. One or both parties may be so adamant even in private sessions with the mediator that all chances of agreement are foreclosed. Here, too, but for different reasons, the mediator may opt to call a joint session. The purpose of the joint session may not only be to report the lack of progress; the mediator may wish to castigate both parties for their intransigence and to underscore the need for movement or compromise on the particular issue if there is to be agreement on other matters or on the contract as a whole. The mediator may go further and spell out the "chamber of horrors" of what may happen if there is continued adamancy on the issue in question. In the most glaring cases of party obstinacy the mediator may feel called upon to express feelings of personal ineffectiveness and threaten withdrawal from the dispute unless one or both of the parties revises its position and provides a meaningful reason for his continuance in the case.

When a party has its first opportunity in joint session to assess the reaction of the other team to the admonitions of the mediator, its realization of the other team's determination may stimulate a rethinking of position and some movement toward settlement. Assessments of the other team's attitudes on specific issues in these joint sessions tend to be more important than at the initial joint session. That is because a specific subject has now been under discussion for a period of time; each party has been lectured by the mediator on the necessity of adjusting its position; and now for the first time the team has seen for itself the adamancy of the other team, reinforcing the mediator's reports in earlier team caucuses.

Teams do tend to become too attached to their positions and too much captive of their own rhetoric to make those timely alterations that are a prerequisite to settlement. The joint session, by revealing that both teams are being comparably stubborn, often provides the stimulus needed for reexamination of positions and moves toward compromise.

If movement does not occur, the mediator still need not declare the mediation process at an end. The stalemate may be a function of team myopia, a transitory failure to adequately recognize the teams' interdependence and need to compromise. Time may heal such shortsightedness, and a break in the mediation may be helpful to all concerned. It provides an opportunity for reflection and assessment by both teams, and for the teams to report back to their principals about the stalemate and to secure new instructions. Probably most important, it gives everyone in the process an opportunity to cool down from the fever pitch of the fruitless confrontation.

———— Encouraging a Return to Direct Negotiations ————

There are times when either of the foregoing extremes (agreement on a number of issues or statemate on all) might persuade the mediator that the parties should return to direct negotiations.

In the former case, the movement of the parties in the direction of settlement and their cooperation in breaking deadlocks on certain matters might mean that they really had no need for mediation. It may also be that the problem which precipitated mediation has been resolved. The responsible mediator may then conclude that it is desirable, as well as more efficient, for the parties to negotiate between themselves without intervention by a third party. If so, the indicated course is withdrawal, together with an offer to return if direct negotiations bog down or if the movement toward settlement provides illusory. Once out, the mediator should stay away for as long as direct negotiations prove fruitful.

If the parties appear reluctant to return to direct negotiations, the mediator can often nudge them in that direction by suggesting that the teams or their leaders chat for a while among themselves, perhaps over dinner or during a coffee break. A more drastic approach is for the mediator to plead unavailability for several days and suggest the teams try to make some movement on their own in the interim.

A stalemate may also provide good grounds for returning the parties to direct negotiations. The mediator may reason that things are going so badly that direct confrontation could not make them any worse; perhaps the teams will recognize the futility of intransigence and the necessity for more cooperative bargaining. The mediator might arrange for the parties to try one or two sessions on their own as a last-ditch effort to stimulate movement before declaring the mediation a failure. Should they need help in that effort, the mediator would be prepared to return—but only if progress was being made toward settlement.

Creating Subcommittees

A joint session may also serve another purpose, that of altering the focus of negotiations from the teams to subcommittees. This may occur when there is agreement between the parties upon a principle or concept but not upon exact terminology. Such smaller groups may be important if not essential to prevent oral understandings from becoming unstuck. The mediator may request at the joint session that each team designate one or two members to meet together. These persons then put into writing the concepts that have been agreed upon and report their recommendations to their respective teams for approval and final agreement on the exact language. If the subject matter is complex, a number of items can be worked on simultaneously. The use of such subcommittees frees the spokespersons from the time-consuming yet important task of drafting language embodying the conceptual settlement, permitting them to devote their attention to other crucial unresolved issues.

The subcommittee may also be a useful device for expediting consideration of many-faceted subjects, such as eligibility for certain types of leave, verification of seniority lists, or the costing of proposals. Persons with special expertise in the areas in question can be assigned to such subcommittees without hindering the flow of the negotiations on the other major issues. The subcommittee concept also permits greater participation of team members, giving them a sense of involvement and responsibility.

The subcommittee approach may also be useful in the event of a stalemate. It enables the mediator to avoid closing off the mediation by assigning stalemated issues to a subgroup. In some cases the mediator may be able to suggest the makeup of the subcommittee, thus bypassing the hostile or obstructive team spokesperson. The subcommittee can be a dangerous device if it is composed of the wrong people or if its recommendations are rejected. Yet if it is successful in breaking the stalemate, it may get the mediation back on track.

The Disruptive Joint Session

The joint session may be an effective tool for the mediator who exercises adequate control over the session. It may prove an ideal medium for announcing the mediator's assessment that the parties are getting along so well they should really go it alone without the mediator. It may help to expedite the mediation by delegating to joint subcommittees the working out of specific language. It may even be a way for the mediator to shift negotiating authority away from the designated team spokesperson. It may, alas, be the forum for the mediator's pronouncing the demise of the mediation effort.

All these possibilities presuppose a purposeful mediator and two pliant and cooperative constituencies. A more exasperating or even volatile result is also possible. The hostility between the parties, the resentment by one party at the other side's failure to move or adjust positions, may be manifested at the joint session. So too may be one or both parties' bitterness toward the mediator for failing to persuade the other side or for failing to get the negotiations moving in any direction.

A harsh word, an ill-timed statement, or even a misunderstood or misinterpreted aside can stir the parties into a raucus confrontation. Such behavior may still be beneficial if it causes each side to appreciate the depth of conviction of its opposite number or at least to appreciate the frustration experienced by the mediator in previous shuttling between teams. Nonetheless, the mediator, if not the parties, should make efforts to avoid it, or to minimize it if it does occur.

Such outbursts should not be tolerated, and the mediator should cut them off as rapidly as possible by sending the teams back to their own sessions, admonishing both for their lack of cooperation. If the mediator is to continue to enjoy the confidence of both teams, however, no individual or side must be held to be at fault. Rather, the mediator should state a refusal to take part in, or tolerate, such behavior and leave the room. When I have had occasion to do this, I have left with the admonition that I won't be party to such childishness. I then wait outside for a few minutes for the parties to calm down and jointly ask me to return. If such a request is not forthcoming then, I will consider the mediation concluded. In all instances there has been a rapid rethinking of position by the party causing the disruption, a return to calm or an apology, and no need to terminate my role as mediator. Tempers do flare and the mediator must be be prepared for that eventuality. To avoid becoming embroiled in the crossfire and to maintain or reassert control over the mediation process is a challenge to any mediator. Sometimes it is useful to permit or even encourage the spokespersons to blow off steam, but the mediator must be careful not to lose control—of personal emotions or of the joint session.

Ending the Joint Session

When the mediator concludes that all possible benefit has been extracted from a joint session, it is time for its dissolution. Termination may be occasioned by an outburst that the mediator may fear will be responded to in kind and threaten escalating hostility, to the detriment of the whole mediation process; too heated an exchange might hinder movement toward settlement. Or the mediator may recognize that nothing beneficial is being accomplished, that the statements of spokespersons are repetitive, and that the teams are merely spinning their wheels. Again, one of the parties may state a new position or basis for compromise to which the other party fails to respond, and the mediator may wish to explore the offer further with either the proposing or the nonresponding party. Sometimes the mediator will end a joint session to prevent one side from taking a step that may foreclose further movement. Such an occasion might occur when one of the parties starts to outline a "final position" when the spokesperson for that team has confided to the mediator that additional movement is possible.

To end a joint session, the mediator may state that it is time to return to separate meetings, indicating which team he will meet with next. Or the mediator may announce a break for a meal, or even an extended suspension of the mediation sessions, with or without a date certain for resumption. Finally, the mediator may withdraw from the case or announce that the mediation is over. Which choice the mediator makes depends on the attitude of the parties and the sensitivity, determination, and/or availability of the mediator. In deciding between continuance and cessation, the mediator must weigh a variety of factors, such as the commitment of the two teams toward continuing, the hour, the length of time devoted to the mediation, contractual deadlines (real or contrived), the benefits (or failures) that might result from the parties separating and meeting with their principals and reassessing their positions, and the impact on the media and the public. The mediator also must consider his own acuity and stamina, ability to remain alert and in control, and future availability and usefulness.

Summary

The joint session of the teams is a valuable tool for the mediator to employ at one or more stages in the mediation. Its primary purpose is to confirm to the parties what has been taking place in the separate sessions between which the mediator has been shuttling. But it also provides the opportunity for each side to reassess the postures taken by the opposite team. In that context it gives the mediator a unique opportunity to determine what course the mediation should take. It might also, however, provide the evidence necessary to conclude that further mediation is futile.

12

SOME PROBLEMS IN MEDIATION

Mediation proceeds with a combination of separate sessions with the teams, with the spokespersons alone or together, and with the teams jointly. The mediator is the maestro, determining which forum is the most conducive to forward movement, which is the most pertinent to the particular moment, and which would best meet the desires of the parties.

In attempting to further the process, mediators are constantly confronted with both substantive and procedural problems which may impede the orderly flow they would like to encourage. Sometimes these problems threaten to jeopardize the entire mediation. Even calling a session with the wrong side at the wrong time may result in claims of favoritism and a threat to leave by the other party. Some of these problems have already been referred to in the context of the joint and separate meetings. But there are other problems that arise throughout the mediation that should be anticipated. They arise in both separate and joint sessions, and tend to be fairly regular in occurrence. Let us look to some of these.

"It's the Other Side's Turn"

The adversary nature of the negotiation process encourages an alternating of presentations, with one side proposing and the other side reacting with a counterproposal, followed by a further counterproposal by the first side. The expectation is that with each volley in this ping-pong match the positions become closer until the teams ultimately arrive at a point where one of the counterproposals will be acceptable to the other team and the issue in dispute will be settled.

This process of exchanging proposals commences in direct negotiations and is continued in the mediation process. The mediator who shuttles back and forth between the teams with proposals and counterproposals enhances the expectation of a response to every proposal.

Such a process will lead to agreement if the parties start at equal distances from the final settlement, and then make an equal number of moves of the same quantum. Thus, if the union opens with a demand for a 20-percent increase, and the employer opens by proposing that wages be frozen or no increase, a series of exchanges with each side altering its prior position by 2 percent would result in agreement on a 10 percent increase in five exchanges. Settlement would also be reached if the union were to reduce its demand in 3-percent steps while the employer raised its offer by 1 percent with each move; agreement would come at 5 percent.

Reaching the End Too Soon

The problem comes when the two sides do not make such symmetrical moves, or when one side arrives too soon at the other's firm position.

If the union started out at 20 percent and the employer began by proposing a wage freeze for the forthcoming contract period, one would expect that with consistent movements the teams would ultimately reach a settlement somewhere in the middle between their opening positions. If settlements elsewhere are about 7 or 8 percent, the savvy union team will space its steps to leave room for both parties to arrive at the magic figure simultaneously. But if the employer is unable or unwilling to meet the prevailing settlement pattern, or if the politics of the union do not permit appropriate reductions, there can be problems.

Take the case where the employer decides that the cat and mouse game of traditional negotiations is passé. At the start of negotiations it reveals to the union that it has had some budgetary problems but nevertheless will do the best it can to match settlements elsewhere, which appear to be in the range of 6 to 7 percent. In its initial proposal it offers a 6-percent increase. The union comes in with a request for an 18-percent increase. After a number of sessions in direct negotiations the employer has come up to 6.1 percent, 6.3 percent, and 6.5 percent. The union has come down from 18 percent to 15 percent to 14 percent to 13 percent. The parties are now in mediation. The mediator begins with the union at 13 percent and the employer at 6.5 percent.

The union alters its position to 11 percent. The mediator relays that message to the employer, which responds with 6.7 percent. The union comes back with 10 percent and the employer responds that it has gone as far as it can, that it has reached the bottom line it had earlier set for itself. It has come as close to 7 percent as its budget allows, and it will not make any more moves until the union gets much closer.

A mediator who takes the message "the employer won't move" to a union that has moved substantially from its opening position is likely to be confronted with the allegation that the other party's refusal to respond with a further move constitutes bad-faith bargaining. The mediator may sense or even know in confidence that the employer has a bit more room for movement. The union either started too high or made movements that were not large enough. Maybe the problem was that the employer came too close to its final position too quickly. Perhaps if the parties had realized where they would wind up they would have behaved differently, but the game can't be replayed. Therefore, the mediator is faced with the problem of the employer's refusal to make a counteroffer and the union's refusal to make two consecutive offers.

Mediator's Choices

The mediator has several choices to extricate the parties from their predicament. The easiest and least rewarding is to castigate each side for its short-sightedness and inexperience in playing the game. More to the point would be to tell the union that a little more may be attainable but the employer is loath to put its final figure on the table until it is sure it will be acceptable. The mediator could then try to exact from the union its final salary proposal in the hope that it would be close enough to that of the employer to induce an acceptance. The mediator would have to make clear that this is not a matter of bad-faith bargaining but rather a case of the employer's having in good faith moved too close to its final position before the union had moved close enough to *its* final position. The union team must be persuaded that the employer's final offer will be made only if the union makes another proposal within range of where the employer is willing to go.

The mediator could also seek to induce the employer team to come up with a counterproposal. The counterproposal might represent little movement and might be calculated to make it clear to the union that it is nearly at the end of the negotiating road. For instance, the employer might propose a small additional flat dollar amount beyond the percentage on the table, or raise the percentage slightly while reducing the monetary value of other items in the package such as health insurance by the same amount. The implication that the union will wind up paying for any further increase by the surrender of other benefits may persuade the union that the employer will yield no more. The more such proposals there are showing the employer's commitment to hold the line, the clearer will be the message to the union. At that point the union will have the option of accepting the employer offer, reducing its proposal to induce an acceptable counter offer from the employer, or insisting on its last proposal and running the risk of escalating the impasse to a strike if the employer fails to concede.

Prohibited Subjects of Bargaining

The issue of excluded subjects of bargaining does not arise often in private-sector collective bargaining. The parties in the private sector are usually sufficiently sophisticated and experienced in negotiations to know what subjects are permitted, as well as what subjects will be viewed as negotiable. In the public sector, by contrast, there are many statutes, ordinances, and judicial and administrative rulings that determine what is and what is not within the scope of the parties' authority to negotiate. Since public-sector bargaining is considered to have evolved from the permission of the sovereign, the sovereign is the authority for determining the issues over which public employers and unions may or may not bargain.

The legislatures, the courts, and the administrative agencies are not loath to tell the negotiators what is permissible and what is not. Nevertheless, the issue of nonnegotiability may well be raised during the mediation. The parties in the public sector frequently become embroiled in arguments over whether a matter is a mandatory, permissive, or prohibited subject of bargaining. There is no problem if the parties agree that an issue is mandatory or permissive and undertake to bargain on it. The problem arises when one of the parties insists on negotiating a subject which the other side insists is nonnegotiable.

Sometimes when a dispute over nonnegotiability is unresolved the parties will agree to abide by the determination of the mediator as to whether something is or is not negotiable. They thus place the mediator in the role of arbitrator with respect to that issue. More often, however, the party insisting that an issue is not negotiable will be unwilling to submit the question to a mutually designated third party for decision. In any event, a ruling by the mediator might well be futile. A mediator/arbitrator has no authority to hold negotiable something that has been excluded from negotiations by law or the courts. A ruling purporting to do this could be readily appealed and overturned.

Mediators should avoid placing themselves in a position where they must interpret the law. They have no authority to issue final and binding interpretations of the law, even if designated as arbitrators by the parties. Moreover, if they undertake to do so they abandon their role as facilitators to become decision makers. Clearly their rulings will be adverse to one of the parties, and the result very likely will be to diminish or destroy faith in the mediator's neutrality. And even if the losing party agrees to conform to the mediator's ruling, the potential for future judicial reversal remains. That is bound to affect adversely the mediator's continued acceptability to and credibility with one or both of the parties.

Other Approaches

Another possible approach for the mediator is to offer to suspend the mediation pending a ruling from the appropriate governmental authority on the issue of negotiability. That approach could result in excessive delay, however, and could force off the table an issue that was of obvious concern to the party seeking to discuss it. In addition, that party would be antagonized at the other party's having resorted to a legal bar against discussing it. The mediator caught in the middle of such a dispute must weigh these considerations, while at the same time respecting the right of a party to decline to discuss a subject which it believes the law makes nonnegotiable.

The mediator who is committed to helping the parties resolve disputes on their merits and is anxious to avoid legalistic impediments might be able to use mediation to secure discussion of a nonnegotiable issue. For example, if, as is usually the case, it is the employer that is refusing to discuss an issue, the mediator might try to persuade the employer that the substance of the issue is so important to the union that ducking it will make matters worse and might even jeopardize settlement chances. The mediator might suggest that the employer discuss the issue on the merits while reserving its right to challenge negotiability before the appropriate forum at a later date.

The mediator might also try to persuade the employer, if it makes no difference to it on the matter of principle, to convert its position of "no" on negotiability to one of "no" on the merits. I have often been successful in this approach, using the analogy that as children we found it more frustrating to hear a parent say, "No, I will not discuss that," than to have the parent explain why my desires on the substantive issue were not attainable. It is unassailable that the purpose of mediation is to resolve disputes, that the union entered the mediation with a problem it wished to have resolved, and that holding that problem nonnegotiable does not confront, let alone resolve, the problem. The mediator should endeavor to have all substantive issues placed on the table for discussion, even those that technically should not be there. Claiming that issues are barred from inclusion in a collective bargaining agreement does not alter the fact that they are issues in the perception of at least one team.

Another way of approaching this problem is to have the moving party acknowledge the nonnegotiability of the issue and then seek to persuade the other party to "discuss" (not "negotiate") the issue, perhaps off the record, perhaps in a separate caucus or meeting, and perhaps apart from the main negotiations. If the parties should reach agreement on the merits of the issue, it can be reflected in a separate letter of understanding or statement of intent.

Whatever the guise, the mediator acts correctly in seeking to have the substantive issue resolved, thus avoiding any escalation of hostility while meeting the main goal of the process: conflict resolution.

Contract Language to Resolve Grievances

It is not uncommon in mediation for either or both parties to seek to use the negotiation process to correct problems encountered in living with prior contract language. No one questions the right of either party to seek "improvements" or "clarification" in contract language that has produced results contrary to its liking. But too often the negotiation process is used to change language that has not yet been tested through the grievance procedure. One or both parties become bent on utilizing the negotiation forum rather than the grievance procedure to make sure their respective interpretations prevail.

Unions sometimes place on the table individual complaints, rather than appeal them through the grievance and arbitration system. By accepting individual claims of alleged wrong as elements of its proposals, the union distracts both the employer and the mediator from more important issues of universal application and unit-wide implication. The focus becomes fixed on issues that are so personalized and so unusual that they may never arise again. Also, in taking such an approach the union risks adverse changes in contract language that is otherwise generally favorable and in arbitration might cause the grievance to be upheld. Thus the union risks loss of substantial benefits when it reopens broad language in order to secure a limited benefit for a member. Moreover, the grievant may lose access to the grievance procedure as well because the grievance no longer is timely.

Dangers of Negotiating Grievances

The mediator can usually spot the grievance that is presented as a legitimate contract demand. The appearance of such a grievance in negotiations may be attributable to internal politics or to frustration with the grievance and arbitration system. Whatever the motivation, the mediator must not permit grievances to be introduced as a way of bypassing and overriding the arbitration procedure and turning the negotiations into a grievance forum. The exception to that rule is the joint willingness of the parties to negotiate a backlogged arbitration agenda by trading off or buying off a number of pending grievances.

Certainly the grievant faced with a loss in arbitration might be able to salvage something in negotiations. And there is no question that a grievance is indeed a dispute between the parties. If the mediator is committed to facilitating settlement by resolving pending disputes between the parties, grievances cannot be ignored any more than non-negotiable issues can. Yet a different standard is applicable to grievances. The parties already have a negotiated procedure for their resolution—the grievance and arbitration system. The parties, particularly the union, risk erosion of the negotiated system, diversion of energy necessary to their negotiation and mediation process, and a loss of faith in both systems if neither proves effective and efficient. With that perspective, the mediator should seek to persuade the parties, usually the union, to divert such complaints back to the grievance procedure, removing them from the list of negotiating demands.

On occasion an individual grievance finds its way into the negotiations because the union failed to invoke the grievance machinery in timely fashion and is unable to secure a waiver of the time limits to return the case to the grievance procedure. It should be noted that, despite the desirability of having such grievances resolved in the correct forum, parties do jointly and willingly on occasion use the negotiations forum to dispose of a number of pending grievances. If the parties both are willing to negotiate the resolution of such grievances, it is the mediator's responsibility to assist them in that effort. In some mediations, grievances do not arise until the end of the process, when they may be considered by the parties as a "sweetener" to secure accord on the entire agreement. The settlement of grievances in such fashion is considered by many to be an expensive method of smoothing ruffled feathers.

Timing

When something is said may often be of greater importance than *what* is said or *how* it is said. This is particularly true in negotiation and mediation. The parties and the mediator must always be alert to the importance of timing. Unfortunately, the skill of correct timing or of using time to advance the mediation itself comes only with time. Experienced parties as well as the experienced mediator develop a keen sense of timing only after they have been guilty of bad timing in earlier dealings.

Too Rapid Movement

From the viewpoint of the parties, moving to the final position on an issue too rapidly can create problems where none need arise, as indicated earlier in this chapter. Such movement may convey the wrong message. It may send a signal to the other side that the party is not really serious about the issue or expects little. Ground lost in the process is virtually impossible to recover.

Movement toward the opposition's position too rapidly may lead that side to think the moving party is about to surrender the whole issue. The moving party may have something altogether different in mind, but the impression of a give-away may be hard to correct. Take the case of a union proposal that every teacher be provided with a private office, which the union revises first to two offices for every three teachers, then to one office for every two teachers, and finally to one office for all teachers in a school building. Too rapid changes in position may persuade the employer that the proposal is not a serious one. The union may really want an office in each school building to which the teachers can repair during their free periods, but by moving too rapidly may have lost its chance to achieve its bottom-line objective.

Holding Out Too Long

By the same token, a party creates a problem by adhering too long to a position that it knows it will ultimately drop. The message to the other side is that that issue, which in fact may be trivial to the proposing party, is a high priority item. The result may be to preclude a response that would otherwise have been forthcoming on other items.

Take the case of an outright ban on subcontracting. The union may have put that unattainable goal into its proposals only because of pressure from a few of its members in the maintenance department. Yet the employer, seeing the proposal remain on the table and having calculated the cost in overtime and equipment purchase of agreeing to it, may hold back on offering costly improvements in the health care package. Not seeing the expected health care benefit proposal after a long series of mediation sessions, the union may conclude that it will not be forthcoming and move to end the mediation, unaware that its adherence to the subcontracting ban is the stumbling block.

Faced with such a standoff, the mediator should recognize that there has been a timing problem and urge the union to reconsider its list of proposals to see if any items can be dropped to induce movement by the other side and to avoid aborting the mediation. Constant monitoring of the items on the table is crucial to the progression of the mediation. The parties should be aware that the ritual fire dance of mediation dictates certain timely releases, withdrawals, and modifications if the process is to end in agreement.

In the Mediator's Pocket

From the mediator's position, it is helpful to know early in the procedure whether a position is firm, amendable, or a throwaway. The mediator in whom the teams have sufficient confidence to provide that information can be helpful with the timing. Knowledge that something will be surrendered at a later time gives the mediator leverage in dealing with the other team. The mediator is described as having that next move "in his pocket." With such information the mediator can, without violating any confidence, provide the other side with gentle, even imperceptible hints as to the fate of a particular proposal. Although the mediator may not be free to reveal his knowledge until authorized to do so by the team providing it, it can still be used effectively. In the case of the subcontracting demand, the mediator might be able to advise the employer unwilling to propose health care improvement that the subcontracting demand "may not be for as much as it appears," or that "I think I might be able to do something on that." At the very least, the mediator could ask, "Do you want to try putting your health care proposal on the table making it contingent on withdrawal of the subcontracting ban?" or even, "If I can talk the union into dropping the subcontracting proposal, would you respond by placing your health care proposal on the table?"

Mediator's Role

The mediator's sense of timing may not always induce the parties to move. Indeed, that sense of timing may impede movement. If the mediator senses that an exchange between the parties is becoming too volatile, it may be prudent, to avoid the cessation of the mediation, to turn the discussion to other items of a less incendiary nature. On the other hand, there may be times when the mediator senses that it is time to move from trivia to crucial issues. The mediator may feel that it is time for the parties to discuss a particularly volatile issue, perhaps after a pleasant dinner together or after there has been satisfactory movement on one or more of the minor issues.

The mediator, more than the parties, is or should be aware of the implications of every movement, and of the anticipated response. To announce a proposal before the other team is receptive is to risk not only increased hostility but also, more important, the loss of an opportunity for progress that might never recur in the same form. Only the mediator, with feet in both camps, is placed to take best advantage of the timing opportunities that arise in the mediation. Precipitate action or tardiness may destroy the mediator's effectiveness.

Good timing may be the key to settlement. Beyond determining what is the most propitious moment for proposing a move or a change of position or a trading of proposals, the mediator must also be alert to timing pressures imposed by the parties.

Reaching the Limit of Team Authority

When the parties prepare for negotiation and mediation, it is not unusual for them to misjudge the intensity of resistance to their proposals, and to assume that they will be able to achieve agreement at a point short of the limit of the other side's authorization. As a consequence they authorize their teams to negotiate to an assumed final point, presumably one with which they are comfortable. The result of an inadequate grant of authority frequently is that the team does not possess the authority to move beyond a particular point. When that point is reached, the mediation comes to a stop.

The problem exists more often on the management side than on the union side. The rank and file of the union will usually give its negotiating team unlimited authority to act on its behalf. The control of the rank and file rests in its power to reject any agreement made by the team through the ratification process. As a result, the negotiating team operates under the threat of nonratification. If it goes too far the settlement may be rejected, and team members may themselves be subject to sanctions, including loss of union office.

On the management side, in contrast, the team is likely to be on a shorter leash, with advance authorization from higher management to go only so far on a proposal. Such limited authorization is justified on the ground that the employer has a limited budget with only so much money to spend. Further, management must be concerned about adequate funding for other aspects of the operation and for the other bargaining units with which it must negotiate comparable benefits. Management in the public sector is also particularly vulnerable to having its internal workings leaked to the other side. For that reason, too, authorization to its negotiating team is often fed in small increments to avoid the risk that word of a higher authorized figure for settlement might be leaked.

Take the case of a management team authorized to agree to a salary increase of 3 percent. The mediator, convinced that 3 percent is as far as the employer's team can go, has persuaded the union to reduce its demand to 5 percent. The union refuses to drop below that figure. The mediator will try the usual ploy to verify that the bottom line of authorization has been met: "You mean that if I got the union to agree to 3 percent plus $10, you could not agree to that settlement?"

If the answer is in the affirmative and shows the team lacks authority to negotiate further, the mediator has the choice of so advising the union, of terminating the mediation, or of focusing his efforts on the management team. The message to management is that agreement is not attainable at the 3 percent figure and that a choice has to be made. First, the employer could adhere to the 3 percent figure and risk an end to the mediation; second, it could negotiate beyond the 3 percent limit and hope for approval of the final settlement; or third, it could seek authorization to go beyond the 3 percent limit.

Teams involved in mediation, despite their differences over the issues being negotiated, generally have a positive attitude toward the mediation process and do not want to disrupt it. They are sensitive to the needs and problems confronted by the other party, and are eager to reach agreement. Restrictions imposed on their negotiating authority by superiors are often frustrating to both teams. There is little likelihood that a team will risk ending talks if it senses that a favorable settlement is attainable just beyond the figure it is authorized to offer.

It is far more likely that the team will choose one of the other options. It is not unusual for a spokesperson to say, "We are authorized to go to X. If we can get agreement at X plus a little, then I am sure it will be approved by our superiors. I can't promise it, but I'll certainly fight hard for approval." The mediator will usually accept that assertion, but he can never really be sure whether the limit of authority has in fact been reached.

Perhaps the highest levels of management have given secret authorization to go beyond X. Whether this is so is unimportant if the team is willing to proceed beyond the stated authorization. The team as a rule can do so since any settlement is subject to ratification and acceptance by both parties. The suspicious mediator may believe that the stated limitation is a ploy, used to persuade the other side that it is wresting from the management more than management really intended to give, while implying that going too far beyond that limitation will increase the risk that higher management will disavow the agreement. Regardless of the motivation and the potential consequences, the mediator is able to continue his efforts to secure a settlement acceptable to the teams.

A different strategy is called for when the management team takes the position that it cannot negotiate beyond the authorized limitation. The role of the mediator, if he is persuaded that the union will not settle at the limitation but might do so at a slightly higher figure, is to urge the management team to avoid loss of a potential settlement by securing authorization to exceed the limitation. The mediator can do this in any of several ways. One way is to urge that the superiors be called into the mediation to see for themselves how close the settlement is and that a bit more on the table may bring agreement. A second possibility is for the mediator to ask the team to secure the additional authorization, breaking the mediation to give it time to contact the superiors by telephone or to meet with them.

Third, the mediator can himself meet with the superiors. Some mediators are unwilling to inject themselves into the realm of internal party relationships. They fear that such intermeddling will undermine the authority of the team and its spokesperson. There is the further risk of antagonizing the team; if successful in securing additional funding or authorization, the mediator must deal with a team that may feel it has been undercut. Other mediators, viewing the achievement of a settlement as more important than maintaining their standing with the particular team, insist on meeting with the higher levels of authority. Frequently the team or its spokesperson obviates the problem by stating that it would appreciate the mediator's trying to expand its authority and volunteering to arrange a meeting with the superiors.

Tardily Raised Issues

The typical mediation proceeds on the basis of the list of issues the parties agreed were in dispute following direct negotiations. Debate between the two teams is limited to those items, and the tardy introduction of other items is precluded. Yet there are occasions when one of the parties feels compelled to introduce a new issue. Unfortunately this usually occurs when the mediator thinks all is going well and that the mediation is drawing to a successful close.

The stimulus may be a realization by a team that is losing that it had better try to salvage something even though the item in question was not earlier considered in negotiations. On the other hand, the party that believes it is "winning" may seek to secure a benefit that was not on its initial roster of demands. Or a party, reviewing its proposals and the negotiating history, may decide that it needs to flesh out a tentative agreement to make sure that all elements are clear and firm before the final agreement is reached.

Tentative Agreements

The term "tentative agreement" is usually applied not only to items agreed to but items that have been withdrawn. The practice of initialing tentative agreements helps to avoid subsequent conflicts as to their status. Nevertheless, there can be misunderstandings over whether an item was agreed to or withdrawn, and in such cases a party may seek to reintroduce an item that was tentatively withdrawn. The mediator may then caution the moving party that such reintroduction will lessen its credibility with respect to tentative agreements and cause the other party to reintroduce items that it had withdrawn.

If the mediator is unsuccessful in persuading the moving party to abandon the item in question, it may be prudent to induce the other party to accept the item as live. Strictly speaking, a tentative agreement is subject to reconsideration if the parties fail to agree on a total settlement; experience shows that discarded items are likely to reappear on the table toward the end of the mediation, as a party seeks to save face or to secure a "sweetener" in the final package. There may be willingness to reconsider small items, but firm resistance to the reintroduction of major items can be expected.

New Proposals

A different situation arises when one of the parties seeks to raise a genuinely new issue that was not considered either during the direct negotiations or earlier in the mediation. Sometimes, it is true, parties forget to make proposals when they are supposed to. A sheet of paper may be overlooked, the person reading the list of proposals may miss a paragraph, or an item that is thought by one side to be related to an item on the table is challenged as a new item by the other side, which then seeks to exclude it from discussion.

The mediator must try to persuade the moving party to drop its new proposal, or the objecting party to rescind its objection. Here, too, the magnitude of the proposal will probably determine whether it will be permitted on the table. A minor issue, such as the resolution of a pending grievance, might be tolerated. More important issues, particularly those involving additional expenditure of funds will meet stronger resistance.

The mediator's success in gaining acceptance of a new issue may also depend upon whether the omission was an oversight and the status of the relationship between the parties. If there is good rapport and a commitment to mutual accommodation, it may be easier to gain acquiescence to a necessary face-saver than if the relationship is a hostile one. The chance that such a problem may arise on either side through oversight, in complete good faith, underscores the importance of the teams separating their personal feelings from their professional responsibilities.

Political Issues

The cooperative nature of the negotiating and mediating process virtually dictates that professional responsibilities not be allowed to erode good personal relationships. Either party may find itself in a situation where it needs the other's assistance to extricate itself from a political problem. Unfortunately, such cooperation makes sense in theory, but frequently cannot be achieved in the face of the intense atmosphere and high stakes of the mediation. Nonetheless, the teams and the mediator should be sensitive to an honest error made in omitting an issue. Both sides should acknowledge the risk of error and recognize that sympathetic handling of it now may prevent its upsetting the whole settlement or the failure of ratification because the error was not allowed to be corrected.

To avoid embarrassment and charges of bad faith and of being misled, the mediator should minimize discussion of an honest error. He should speak only to the two spokespersons and request an accommodation to the error.

One solution may be for the parties to agree to soft pedal the issue involved, leaving it as a matter to be handled at the end of the mediation through some face-saving measure such as its inclusion in a later package proposal, or by its grant as a final sweetener.

Overlapping Offers

In the best of all possible worlds mediation will be so successful that the parties will respond to a request for their best offers by providing final positions. If that brings them to the same figure, the mediator has no problem. But what if the parties make overlapping offers to the mediator, i.e., the employer offers to pay more than the union offers to accept?

Mediators differ on how to deal with this admittedly infrequent problem. Some suggest that the mediator should split the difference and announce to both parties a settlement that is halfway between the two offers. Initially each side will be pleased—the employer will have saved money, while the union will have obtained more than it was willing to settle for. But afterwards the parties are bound to talk and discover that each could have had a more favorable settlement. From the employer's viewpoint, the mediator could have announced a settlement at the lower figure the union was willing to accept. From the union's viewpoint, the mediator could have announced a settlement at the higher figure the employer indicated it was willing to pay. These after-the-fact discoveries may adversely affect the mediator's future acceptability with both parties. More important, such difference-splitting raises the question of the authority of the mediator to make such a selection of the final settlement figure. Was the mediator exceeding his authority in announcing a figure halfway between the two offers? Would it have been proper to select either of the two offers rather than split the difference? Who authorized the mediator to make a decision for the parties? Isn't the mediator there to help the parties reach their own agreement?

Referral to Parties

The more prudent approach, I suggest, is for the mediator caught in such a wonderful dilemma to announce to the parties jointly that they have reached an area of agreement and should meet directly with each other, without the mediator, to work out the details of their settlement. The mediator should then withdraw, leaving to the parties the task of ascertaining what that settlement should be. The first to make a proposal acceptable to the other side will have shaped the agreement, and the other side, willing perhaps to make a comparable move, will be spared the need to do so. The mediator, of course, will be saved the dilemma of having to opt for one settlement out of several available, and the final solution will remain where it should be, between the parties themselves. The mediator will have done the facilitating, but the parties will have cut the final deal.

Language Problems

It is not unusual for the parties to agree only on a general concept for resolving an issue, particularly after long hours of extended but unsuccessful debate and discussion over language. Of course, it might be desirable for the teams and their future dealings if they spent extra time working out the details and the language of their understanding. But the parties do not always do what is best for them or even what is reasonable. In the euphoria of securing conceptual agreement they tend to minimize or ignore the problems that may arise later in working out the details of that understanding. What initially seemed a perfectly clear settlement in principle may become muddled, particularly if in the subsequent exchanges one of the parties finds itself losing on another issue that it considers important. It may seek to compensate for such a setback by taking a tighter stance with respect to the agreement in principle.

The mediator may find this is a convenient situation in which to use a committee approach. A subcommittee composed of team members who will have to live with the agreed-upon concept might be proposed.

Such individuals are more likely to develop workable language and not to seek political victories.

Sometimes it is not possible to get the preferred people on such a committee, or even to have the matter referred to committee. The task may then have to be undertaken by the teams or their spokespersons. In such a case the mediator may be asked to develop language implementing the agreement in principle, or the mediator might offer to do so if the parties seem to be spinning their wheels. Obviously language proposed by the mediator is advisory. Both parties have the opportunity to evaluate and criticize and accept or reject what the mediator proposes.

Summary

The complexity of the mediation process, the multitudinous details attendant to reaching an agreement, and the adversary character of the relationship mean that problems of many kinds will occur in the course of the mediation. When the parties are unable to resolve those problems, the mediator may have to play a role that is more active than merely shuttling between the parties relaying messages. The more experience the mediator has with the process, the more likely it is that he will recognize such problems and handle them routinely.

Every mediation has some, if not all, of these problems. They may appear to the parties, and even to newer mediators, to be insurmountable obstacles. But, like the issues on the table, they are amenable to resolution, and must be resolved for agreement to be reached. Patience, experience, good faith, and a commitment to achieving agreement are the elements that lead to resolution of these ancillary challenges.

13
MOVING TOWARD SETTLEMENT

There comes a point in the mediation when the parties seem to sense that some of the biggest obstacles have been overcome and that a climate conducive to settlement has set in.

That point may be reached shortly after the outset of the mediation if the parties were deadlocked on one particular issue that was quickly resolved. It may come after the boulder in the road has been pushed aside, if that was the main stumbling block to settlement. But more likely, the big break will occur only after several sessions of hard work relaying proposals, changing packages around, having the peripheral demands withdrawn, and focusing on the biggest issues in dispute between the parties. Once those items are out of the way, settlement psychology, as Eva Robins has termed it, takes effect. That psychology may be the public sector equivalent to the private sector deadline.

Economic Aftermath

For most negotiations the event that starts the "roll" toward settlement is agreement on the money items, particularly wages. The contemporary negotiating scene reveals, however, that other items may constitute the biggest stumbling blocks on the way to settlement. Procedures for reduction in force, guidelines for subcontracting, guarantees against reductions of health benefits, and even provisions for employee retraining have taken center stage.

Once the settlement threshold is reached the parties may be able to take the necessary closing moves on their own, or they may turn to the mediator to orchestrate the movement toward settlement. It should not be assumed that the remaining issues are unimportant, or that they will all be swept off the table. To the contrary, the mediation may be stymied, and indeed may even collapse, if there is a failure to agree on the remaining issues. What has changed, then? The change may be in the team members' perception of the process. In the early stages of the

146

mediation the parties approached it with frustration left over from failing to get their ideas across to the other side in direct negotiations. As the mediation proceeded, new frustrations may have arisen from the other side's refusal to make meaningful concessions or compromises. These frustrations may have been exacerbated by the lack of access to the other team and the necessity of relying on an outsider's reports of the attitudes and reactions of the opposing team. Then suddenly there is agreement on an issue which was the chief source of this frustration. Things seem brighter; the remaining issues, though still important, are not of comparable magnitude to the issue just resolved.

Both parties may experience the change in attitude at the same time on the same issue. But it may also be triggered by different issues for each side, and one party may experience the change before the other does.

Once the parties both feel settlement is at hand, they seem to be more willing to rely on the assistance and to respond to the prodding of the mediator. Perhaps it is because the mediator's assistance was crucial in getting the big problem resolved, perhaps because the parties are not so tense about the remaining, less vital issues, and perhaps because they have had enough and want to end the exercise.

One of the strongest weapons the mediator has at this stage is the fact that the remaining issues tend to be less volatile and less likely to incite the parties to conflict. The big issue, the stumbling block to settlement, is often the biggest strike issue as well. When that is resolved the weaponry for a successful strike or lockout is dissipated. None of the remaining issues is important enough to all of the constituencies to support a strike action. Accordingly, the teams are more likely to gear themselves toward accommodation, and following the advice of the mediator becomes a convenient way of resolving the remaining issues.

The mediator may be called upon to orchestrate the final elements of the settlement. Any suggestions from the mediator for moving to full agreement come from no secret source. They are the standards of conflict resolution used throughout the mediation on all the other elements of the dispute.

Standards for Settlement

Comparability

For the resolution of the remaining issues, the parties frequently embrace standards of comparability. The standard that might be presented by the mediator is the prevailing practice in the area. Thus if most other communities, or all contiguous communities, or communities of like size in the state provided for three days of funeral leave for the death of next of kin, that might be a reasonable standard for the parties. The mediator might point out that if the parties did not resolve the issue themselves and appealed their impasse to fact finding, that number of days might be recommended in any event.

Quantum of Cost

Another standard that generally is acceptable at this stage is the quantum of cost. The parties are realistic enough to recognize that most benefits will add to the cost of the package. Once settlement is reached on the major items such as wage or salary levels, the parties can be expected to be sensitive to the fact that additional cost items may be too expensive. If other cost items were sacrificed to concentrate all available dollars into salary, the parties have a built-in basis for consideration of all subsequent economic items.

A remaining proposal such as, say, subsidized eye glasses might cost 1 percent of total compensation, yet would seem important to only some of the employees. It is unlikely that the union would push hard for such a proposal and thus jeopardize the compensation package. The same would be true for cost items benefiting only a portion of the work force when they came up for discussion following the compensation settlement. Even a much less costly item such as a commitment to provide compensation in lieu of make-up time for errors in the assignment of overtime work is likely to be viewed in the context of its cost.

When compensation has been the big stumbling block in the negotiations, and the parties have endeavored to devote all available funds to the compensation package, there is a fairly effective deterrent to the expenditure of further funds for the cost items among the unresolved issues. The only achievable after-crisis improvements would thus be in the noneconomic realm. But even as to noneconomic items, little leverage can be asserted after agreement has been reached on compensation.

Administrative Matters

Certain of the remaining issues often relate to the administration of the enterprise. Take for instance the issue of dues deduction, a common practice in the private sector but still relatively new in the public sector. With the advent of computers, one often hears the excuse that the employer cannot fit dues deduction onto the computer payroll card.

If such is the employer's excuse, the matter is often solvable by a review of the administrative problem that is asserted. If in fact there is no room for an additional deduction on the payroll card, the problem may be resolved by the elimination of one of the deductions currently being made, or by redesigning the payroll card to permit more deductions. The latter alternative might be objected to because of cost, but perhaps implementation could be deferred until the current stock of payroll cards is exhausted.

If the employer were proposing to require that all uniforms be purchased at a store designated by the employer, one could foresee a union response that this would violate a prior understanding, or infringe upon the employees' personal shopping freedom, or prevent the employees from saving money by purchasing at some other less costly store. Such a discussion could easily lead to a resolution that was administratively acceptable to both sides, encompassing a number of approved stores or the grant of a fixed dollar amount for the purchase of uniforms at the employer-designated store. Or the parties could agree to arrangements for a discount at the employer-designated store to bring the prices into line with those at other, cheaper stores.

In the area of changes in administrative operations, the parties are usually practical enough to work out arrangements which meet their respective needs without making administration unduly burdensome. When faced with such issues, the mediator often will find it helpful to solicit the views of the team members who are involved in the day-to-day problems of administration in the area under discussion for their reactions and proposed solutions to the problems.

Impact on Other Bargaining Units

Frequently the employer will object to a proposal made by the union because of its impact on other bargaining units in the plant or the jurisdiction. This is a frequent employer concern with respect to insurance benefits. Many employers have employer-wide or system-wide insurance plans and are unable to adjust levels of benefits for a single bargaining unit. When such a demand arises, the mediator often points out to the union its lack of authority to alter the benefits for other bargaining units, and the employer's inability to alter the benefits for only one group of covered employees.

It may be possible instead for the employer to provide a similar benefit outside the insurance package. This might be an acceptable solution for the employer if it did not adversely affect the employer's dealings with the insurance carrier, or its contracts with the other bargaining units, and did not destroy the parity of insurance benefits among all of the units. Even a token offering in such a case might be acceptable to the union. Thus, if the union was seeking an eye-care plan when none of the other bargaining units under the universal health insurance program had that benefit, an acceptable alternative might be annual eye examinations on employer time at some city-owned health center.

A similar problem might arise if the employer sought union agreement to eliminate an existing benefit, such as an extra holiday, to put its constituency on a par with other employees. Here the mediator might initially seek union acquiescence to the change, but if unsuccessful might seek to persuade the employer to drop the demand by pointing to bargaining units of similar composition elsewhere that enjoyed the extra holiday.

Other ways of resolving the issue of conformity among bargaining units, include the development of side letters of agreement; a commitment to grant disputed benefits if they are agreed to in contracts covering other units; and a commitment to reopen negotiations if certain triggering events occur in the negotiation of agreements for the other bargaining units.

Contract Duration

In the effort to achieve agreement on substantive contract terms, the issue of contract duration frequently is overlooked. Employer and union may agree in advance on the duration of the contract they are negotiating, but in many cases that, too, is a disputed issue in mediation. In a period of inflation unions prefer short-term contracts so that wage rates are not frozen when higher scales are being negotiated elsewhere. The employer, on the other hand, is likely to desire a long-term contract to avoid the frequent renegotiation of contract terms.

In those cases where duration is unresolved, the contract term itself becomes a valuable tool in the mediator's effort to bring the parties closer together. Following separate sessions with the parties the mediator may be in a position to hold out to the employer the carrot of a longer contract term in exchange for movement on a proposal made by the union. Or the mediator may be able to offer to the employer a desired contract change on condition that it agree to a contract of shorter duration. Duration of the agreement provides the mediator with a temporal tool to be used in conjunction with work on the substantive issues in dispute. It is one of the most commonly used tools in mediation, providing a link between the value of benefits and the value of time.

Expiration Date

The expiration date of the contract being negotiated is another element of contract duration that tends to become a negotiating tool. The parties often think in terms of their next round of negotiations and the impact the agreement being negotiated will have on them at that time. Each wants to place itself in the most favorable position when the next negotiations commence. Sometimes there is a joint concern, to make sure that the contract is wrapped up prior to a budget review date or to continue the present contract until the employer is assured that it will have the funds necessary to underwrite the successor agreement.

Staggering the Benefits

It is the mediator's task to capitalize on the necessity for agreement on duration by using it as a means of achieving agreement on substantive issues. Frequently a compromise that is beneficial to both parties can be worked out. If the agreement is for longer than one year, the parties can use it as a device for introducing different benefits at different times. The mediator may effectively use time as a means of effecting compromise between the parties when there is objection to the introduction of a substantial benefit all at once. Spreading out the introduction of a benefit over the life of the contract may make it more palatable. Thus, employer resistance to a two-day increase in the number of personal leave days might be overcome by providing one additional day at the inception of the agreement and a second day at the start of the second year of the agreement.

Stretched-out introduction of benefits has particular benefit to the parties in the area of wages. To implement a 4-percent increase at the start of the contract would cost 4 percent throughout the life of the agreement and provide a 4-percent increase in earnings. But to provide for 2 percent at the start of the agreement, and the second 2 percent halfway through the agreement would cost only 3 percent over the life of the agreement. Although such delayed implementation would raise employees' earnings over the contract term by only 3 percent rather than 4 percent, it would increase by 4 percent the level from which the next contract talks begin. Staggered introduction of increases reduces the impact on the employer, permitting a greater increase by the end of the agreement than the employer might be willing to grant at the start of the agreement. This approach can in fact provide a higher ending figure at a lower total cost. A 2-percent figure at the start of the agreement, a 1-percent increase at mid life, and a 2-percent increase in the last month of the agreement will cost less than a 4-percent increase throughout the life of the agreement, yet will provide a higher starting point for the next agreement. Smaller total earnings during the life of the agreement may be more palatable to the union if the next round of negotiations will start at a higher level or if the money saved by the employer is used to pay for other cost items on the table. If the mediator is aware of the union's preference as between the immediate benefit and the end figure, the staggering of the increases throughout the life of the agreement can become an important means of moving the parties to settlement on the thorny issue of wages.

The parties can also agree that certain external signals will trigger changes in the contract terms. The most commonly used such signal is the federal government's Consumer Price Index (CPI). Thus, the parties might agree that wages will be increased by a specified percentage on a certain date during the contract term if the CPI has risen by a specified amount by that date.

Each of these variables is a tool for the mediator to use to help bridge the gap between the parties on economic as well as noneconomic issues. Too often the parties, after agreeing on the amount of a wage increase, remain deadlocked as to its distribution. Staggered benefit introduction dates may provide the mediator with the tool for compromise.

Contract Reopener

Sometimes the mediator may not be able to secure firm agreement on the introduction of benefits either at the start of the agreement or at some fixed point during the agreement. Perhaps it will be possible in that situation to persuade the reluctant party to agree to reconsider its position at some later date during the contract term.

The parties may, for example, come to terms on a multiyear agreement on the noneconomic issues, while agreeing to an interim contract reopener on the matter of wages and/or other economic benefits. The subject matter to be discussed during a reopener is a matter for negotiation between the parties, as is the date of the reopener. The union generally will push for a broad reopener; the employer, on the other hand, usually prefers to limit talks to a few issues. Often the mediator can postpone a confrontation on that question by excluding it for the present and making it a subject for discussion during the reopener.

Contract duration is really the equivalent of a promise of peaceful relations for a fixed period of time. Most mediators are aware of the preference of professional negotiators on both sides for a longer rather than a shorter contract term. The astute mediator can distinguish a "no" from a "not now," and a "need now" from a "need during the term" of the agreement. On the basis of such signals the mediator can utilize the timing of the implementation of agreed-upon provisions to help the parties work through their difficulties with substantive matters.

Cost of Subsequent Legal Challenge

The mediator sometimes is faced with a challenge to the legality of a proposal, one party insisting it must have a provision and the other side insisting with equal vigor that the proposal is illegal and will be tested in court if inserted into the agreement. The prospect of subsequent litigation may be turned to advantage by the mediator in the effort to bridge the gap between the parties. If the parties are obdurate, the mediator may have little leverage beyond pointing to the cost of the litigation that might arise from insistence on the insertion of the provision. If it is the employer that is threatening to go to court, the mediator might urge that the potential cost of the litigation be channeled into other benefits as the price for withdrawal of the disputed provision.

The mediator may also be able to suggest alternatives that might be acceptable to the parties. One would be to seek an advisory court opinion on the disputed provision, with the understanding that it would be inserted into the contract if held to be legal by the court. Another would be to write the provision into the agreement, subject to the condition that it would not be effective during any court challenge and be severed from the contract without affecting other provisions if finally declared illegal. Yet another possibility would be to secure agreement to have the disputed provision incorporated into a side letter, or for its content to be implemented without written verification. The mediator might be able to tie a dispute of this type to the issue of contract duration by making the provision effective at a later date during the contract term unless it had been held illegal in the meantime.

Precluding Organizational Rivalry

Most union organizations function with one eye over their shoulder watching to see what a rival union might be doing on their turf. That concern is probably most marked during the negotiation process, when failure to achieve promised levels of benefits or failure to achieve comparability may constitute an open invitation to rival unions to begin or escalate organizational efforts. The risk that there may be a move to replace the incumbent organization is frequently a matter of concern to the employer as well. Employers often would rather live with the enemy they know than risk involvement with an enemy they don't know. The mere prospect of a rival organizational drive threatens not only financial costs for both parties but disruption of operations and animosity within the employee group. Since both parties are likely to wish to avoid such organizational efforts, the mediator is often able to use the prospect of an organizational drive as a tool for settlement. The spectre of a rival union waiting in the wings may be sufficient to induce the employer to forestall its effort to displace the incumbent union by meeting area standards. On the union side fear of being ousted might engender a willingness to shift from one issue to another that has been identified as a goal of the rival group. In this area the mediator who has familiarity with area standards and unionization efforts might prove to be of more assistance to the parties than one who lacks such familiarity.

Stimulating Movement

Even when the parties have recognized that they are in a settlement mode, there are still serious problems for the mediator. Indeed, issues that seemed small or insignificant earlier in the mediation tend to take on a new dimension and become crucial matters. As the anticipated "big" issues are resolved, the parties tend to pay greater attention to the smaller issues and to raise them to a higher priority. Once economic matters are settled the employer feels little pressure to move on other issues, since any strike potential has been diluted. The union, on the other hand, though still troubled by political and other remaining demands, has little leverage for securing them. There appears to be a greater tendency to become stymied by trivia. The mediator often finds it necessary to advise the parties that they are focusing on minuscule matters and jeopardizing their great progress on the bigger issues by accentuating the smaller issues left in dispute. It may even become necessary to point out the risk that the whole settlement may founder over an item that was never before considered to be important.

Faced with a deadlock on the remaining issues, the mediator may find it expedient to meet with the spokespersons to attempt to jolt them into a sense of reality and to rely on their desire for a settlement to help in steering the parties away from the distracting nibbles they are taking at items that should be more readily disposed of. William E. Simkin, a former director of the Federal Mediation and Conciliation Service, suggested that the "nibblers" can be thwarted by announcing agreement in principle on the issues, leaving it to the parties to work out the details after the mediator has left the scene.

Reopened Issues

In addition to the ballooning of the small issues, the mediator is often confronted with another problem—an issue everyone thought was settled comes into focus again because of a matter raised in an ancillary issue. When that occurs the parties may find themselves again discussing elements of an item they had earlier agreed to. It is important that this be done before final agreement is reached, since the confusion might lead to rejection in the ratification process or serious problems in contract implementation.

At this stage the mediator can exert pressure with respect to the remaining issues by invoking the settlement as whole. Each unresolved issue, after all, does jeopardize the broader settlement. To the extent that the conflict at this stage is over the small issues, the parties can usually be jolted back to reality by the risk of losing the big settlement through obstructionist tactics.

Structuring the Package

As the parties continue to deal with the remaining issues, they usually find themselves with a number of unresolved matters. Some are matters of significance over which the parties are really deadlocked. Others are matters that have remained on the table only because of the reluctance of the sponsor to pull them off.

Frequently the parties will put together packages of remaining proposals and positions toward the end of mediation in an effort to wrap things up. A package may be more important for what it omits than for what it includes. If the union has kept on the table a proposal for reimbursed cleaning of uniforms despite repeated employer refusals to agree to it, a package of remaining items that makes no reference to the uniform-cleaning demand may signal a big breakthrough, a tacit acknowledgement that the demand has been dropped. The mediator must keep on top of all the issues, and be aware of what is missing as well as what is included in the various packages.

When a proposed package is rejected, the mediator may be placed in the position of having to recast the package to make it more appealing. From prior exposure to the positions of the other side the mediator may even be able to help in framing a proposal by indicating to the team what is likely to be accepted, what is likely to be rejected, and what is worth trying out to test the other team's reaction. The mediator may in fact be performing the same role for both teams, helping each to put together a package that will prove acceptable to the other side.

Once a package is on the table, or once both teams have assembled and presented their respective packages, the role of the mediator is to nudge the parties toward a common meeting ground, suggesting the trading off of items and the substitution of less objectionable language for phraseology that is causing antagonism.

On occasion the mediator will propose that a particularly thorny issue be submitted to a joint study committee, or that something be dealt with in a separate letter or side agreement. Submission of an issue to a study committee provides the sponsor with recognition that the issue is still alive, while eliminating it as a stumbling block in the negotiations.

Summary

Once the parties have both come to the realization that settlement is attainable, their attitude toward the issues in dispute and toward each other begins to change. Though still seeking to exact the most favorable contract terms from the other side, each side recognizes that none of the remaining issues is significant enough to precipitate a strike or to hold up settlement for very long and that the price of settlement is compromise.

In the process of reconciling their differences, the mediator may utilize a number of different external standards to encourage the casting of the remaining issues in a more acceptable light. Area standards, cost considerations, the administrative problems or benefits presented by a proposal, the impact of a proposal on other bargaining units within the enterprise, considerations of timing, the potential cost of a legal challenge, and the impact of a rival union on the negotiations are among the factors that the mediator may find of use in encouraging the parties to move from intransigent positions to positions of compromise.

By carefully monitoring all the issues that have been on the table, and by suggesting appropriate rearranging and repackaging of proposals, the mediator may move the parties closer to final agreement. Many of the tricks of the mediator's trade are employed to best advantage during this winding down of the mediation process. Agreement may remain elusive during these steps, but it is within reach, and all parties recognize that it is attainable at the right time and with the right packaging.

14

PERSONAL CHALLENGES TO THE MEDIATOR

As the two teams wend their way through direct negotiations, they tend to become so immersed in the issues that conversion to the mediation process and the intervention of the mediator is sometimes viewed as merely the acquisition of a mouthpiece to overcome the frustrations of getting the message across to the other side. The mediator also serves each party as a sounding board for its views and as a vehicle for gaining insight into the other party's reactions. Sometimes the parties become so used to the separation of teams that is the hallmark of the mediation process that they ignore direct communication and rely instead on the mediator to serve as the essential communicator between them.

The successful mediator is the one who can function without affecting the parties' belief that they are still in control of the process. There are times when the parties embrace the suggestions and input of the mediator as their own, ignoring their origin with the "outsider." Most mediators are content with a low profile, preferring the focus to be on the teams. They accept with equanimity or even with a measure of relief their role as conduits rather than the hub of the mediation.

There are times when the focus shifts away from the issues and directly to the mediator. Just as each team is prone to blame the other team for intransigence or even foul play, the teams individually or jointly can vent their wrath against the mediator when something goes wrong, whether or not it was the mediator's fault. Such outbursts can occur when the parties perceive that the mediator has done something wrong, when they are chafing under the working rules the mediator laid down, and at times when conditions totally beyond the control of the mediator require a "scapegoat."

Situations such as these explain why the mediator is supposed to be "thick skinned." The mediator must respond in a manner that is effective in getting the parties to focus again on the issues, and does not prejudice the mediator's effectiveness throughout the remainder of the mediation.

157

A number of such incidents may occur in a mediation, and they should be recognized as being likely to arise despite the greatest care to avoid them. In a small way their occurrence may be an indication that the mediator is at work, occasionally provoking a reaction that shows he or she is more than a part of the woodwork.

Charges of Prejudice Against One Side

The mediator must spend a great deal to time closeted with each team, or meeting in the hall in whispered conversation with one or the other of the spokespersons. Given such intimate contact, it is not surprising if the members of one or both teams suspect collusion. In fact it is a wonder that mediators are able to have such close relationships with the teams and still be acceptable to both sides. Perhaps the fact that mediators seek to gain and retain the confidence of both teams simultaneously accounts for the infrequency of charges of favoritism. Nevertheless, such charges do arise and the mediator must be prepared to respond to them.

Prior Relationships

Sometimes a charge may stem from the fact that the mediator previously mediated or arbitrated with one of the parties. Perhaps the mediator is related to, or a social friend of, a team member. Or the mediator might have discussed some elements of the case socially with one of the spokespersons before being designated as the mediator. To guard against accusations of prejudice, the mediator at the commencement of the mediation should disclose any prior relationship with either of the parties and leave it up to either side to raise an objection to the mediator's continuing in the case. Such a disclosure does not presage a withdrawal by the mediator from the case; it is a matter of explaining prior conduct and leaving it to the parties to decide whether the mediator's impartiality is compromised. The prudent mediator will search his memory carefully to recall any prior contacts in order to avoid their being discovered later by one of the parties, and to avoid a charge that the failure to disclose is itself evidence of prejudice.

It is questionable whether the mediator should reveal all prior professional contacts with one of the parties or its spokesperson. Professionals, whether mediators or spokespersons, are expected to have had experience in the field. In my earlier mediation cases I made a deliberate effort to list prior cases involving one or both of the parties as well as the spokespersons. With more experience I began to assume that the parties were aware of my experience and that in fact, it was a factor in my selection. Now I seldom mention prior professional relationships, although I do seek to work into the initial joint dealings the fact that I have had prior cases with one or both of the parties or spokespersons, leaving it to the parties to raise any questions they wish about the details or frequency of prior relationships.

Sometimes the mediator when selected is unaware of a prior relationship that might cause suspicion. I have been in cases where a call from one of the parties gave me no indication as to who was representing the other side. Yet in one case I discovered at the initial meeting that one party was represented by an old friend with whom I had gone to law school. I made the relationship clear immediately, and offered to withdraw. As in most cases where the mediator is honest in revealing prior relationships, the parties were willing to proceed without protest. Sophisticated parties recognize that the price of selecting experienced mediators is that they may have had prior cases with one or both of the parties. They seem to be able to live with such prior dealings. But they also have a right to expect that the mediator will reveal any relationships other than professional that might be construed by either party as impeding the mediator's effectiveness as a neutral. This is not, after all, an arbitration, in which a prior relationship might influence a decision by which both parties are bound; the mediator has no decision-making power. Furthermore, the parties are free to ask the mediator to withdraw at any time if one or both parties feel there is evidence of prejudice or wrong doing, or simply ineffectiveness.

Charges of Bias

A more serious charge is that of bias in the mediation process itself. Such a charge may arise in a multitude of ways. One party may feel the mediator is spending too much time with the other team, or is deliberately misquoting its proposals in talking to the other side, or is currying favor in order to improve the chances of selection in another case, or as an umpire under the agreement being negotiated or another agreement. Other than a charge of accepting a bribe, of which I have never heard, allegations of prejudice can arise over any behavior of the mediator, real or fancied.

Responding to Charges

What should the mediator do when such a charge is raised? If the charge is one that can be factually rebutted, the mediator should endeavor to do so. The mediator's reputation should be defended, and the confidence of the parties needs to be reestablished., Thus, if the mediator is accused of having deliberately misquoted a proposal, it is a simple matter to bring the parties together and ask what was said, or to read what is in the mediator's all-important notes.

If the charge is not one that can be factually answered, or if a factual answer is not accepted as proof of the mediator's neutrality, the mediator has a more serious problem. One possibility is to attempt to continue to rebut the charge with assertions of innocence. That is often futile, since the impression of prejudice will remain and will be bound to interfere with the mediator's subsequent efforts to serve in a neutral posture.

If the mediator is convinced that suspicion of favoritism persists, the easiest and most forthright approach is to offer to withdraw from the case. In such a situation the mediator should make it clear that he or she bears no animosity toward the charging party, but that a continuing perception of favoritism may render the mediator ineffective. Such a perception might be expected to detract from the mediator's credibility with the party, and hence to impede the progress of the mediation. Both the charging party and the other party, which might fear a compensatory favoritism toward the charging party, should have the opportunity to accept the mediator's offer to withdraw. More often than not a party given such an opportunity will decline to take advantage of it.

In some cases the accusation of prejudice or misconduct may be so strong or so troublesome that the mediator feels uncomfortable or refuses to continue in the case, even if the parties both want such continuation. The mediator may feel that such a charge is irremediable, or so offensive that impartiality will be thereafter impossible. The mediator must feel as comfortable with the parties as they feel with the mediator. A mediator who believes he is mistrusted or suspected of favoritism becomes ineffective. Mediators, too, have egos, and they cannot be expected to perform to their greatest potential if they either do not respect or do not trust one or both parties.

Withdrawal from a case under such circumstances does not usually damage the mediator's reputation or future acceptability. Insistence on remaining in a case when one of the parties does not want the mediator to remain or when the mediator obviously has an antipathy toward one or both of the parties, on the other hand, can do long-term damage to the mediator's reputation. Parties usually recognize that relationships between adversaries and relationships with messengers can lead to misunderstandings and mistrust. They usually respect the mediator who, sensing a loss of confidence on the part of a party, voluntarily withdraws. Such independence and respect for the process is unlikely to have an adverse effect upon the mediator's future acceptability.

Errors and Omissions in Transmission

It should come as no surprise that mediators make mistakes in transmission. They should not, and they do not do so often, but errors do occur. The mediator may cure challenges to credibility by showing that the message in question was accurately transmitted. But what if it was not?

Even though what is proposed is written down with great care, read back for verification, and then read verbatim to the other side, the possibility remains that an error will be made, whether of omission or commission. Sometimes the mediator omits reading a portion of a package proposal because it appears on a different page or under a different clause in the notebook. Sometimes a last-minute change, made as the mediator walked out the door and not written down, is forgotten because of an unanticipated distraction. Sometimes wording in one proposal is inadvertently substituted in another proposal. Such errors do occur. Whether it be minor or major, the mediator must confess to an error. It might assuage the mediator's conscience to explain why the error was made, but the fact remains that a mistake was made; the parties may have acted in reliance upon it; and as a result the mediation may have taken a different turn than if the message had been accurately relayed.

Admitting an Error

Here again the prudent policy is for the mediator to admit the error and to leave to the parties the option of determining, whether the misconduct was so serious that the mediator's acceptability has been jeopardized. The mediator should offer to withdraw from the case if there is any likelihood that the conduct has impaired the mediator's effectiveness. If the misconduct is uncharacteristic and the mediator's performance has been otherwise acceptable, the offer of withdrawal will probably be rejected, and the mediation will be permitted to continue.

Another type of error of transmission is alteration by one of the parties of what the mediator has reported. Sometimes the alteration is deliberate; sometimes it is inadvertent. If the parties are being kept separate, the mediator can usually correct the error before it is compounded by a response. The mediator may catch the error while listening to the discussion of a message, or when a response is given to him for transmittal. Sometimes it is not caught, or is deliberately concealed to avoid discovery by the mediator. In the latter situation the mediator may elect to accept an admission of error or withdraw from the case.

Deliberate falsification of transmittals by a party is rare, but innocent mistakes of hearing, or wishful hearing, do occur. Reiteration of messages can usually avoid such calamities. If they do occur, the mediator should be as forgiving as the parties should be if it were the mediator who erred.

Misquotes in the Media

In most mediations the parties have little difficulty in agreeing to an exclusion of the media from the proceedings and to a ban on communications by the parties to the media. The general practice is to leave the responsibility for media contacts to the mediator, who usually makes a routine daily report of progress without being specific and without revealing anything that might disclose the positions of the parties on disputed issues.

Team Leaks

But media relations do not always comport with the agreed-upon model. Occasionally there are leaks by team members or even by a team spokesperson. Sometimes media representatives may pursue the participants, angling for a lead or to secure an "exclusive" to upstage competition. At other times a reporter may gain access to the internal "hotline" telephone number of employer or union and find out and announce details of positions. Such reports are then denounced as violations of the ban on media contact, with threats to provide the other side of what was reported. It is at this stage that the mediator must enter the fray to prevent the erosion of the media ban and perhaps the destruction of the entire mediation. Unfortunately, when what is reported is favorable to one of the parties, the mediator must try to persuade the other party, the offended side, to refrain from retaliating. This is a difficult task; the mediator must convince the offended party that a response will only escalate hostilities and move the format of the dispute from the mediation chambers to press, radio, and television. A public forum is not the place where the mediator can effectively bring the parties together.

A leak that was accidental is the easiest of situations to deal with. The party responsible presumably is aware of the need for a media freeze, and endorses it. The mediator's only task in that situation is to convince the other side that the leak was inadvertent and to work with the party responsible for the leak to make sure there will be no repetition.

If a leak was deliberate, there is little the mediator can do besides remonstrate with the guilty party, pointing to the risk of escalated public warfare and the danger of shifting the negotiations from the mediation to the media. If the source of the leak was someone other than the spokesperson, the mediator might be successful in persuading the spokesperson to use his or her influence with the team to prevent further leaks.

Mediators are not police officers. They cannot be expected to exercise police powers in a procedure that is voluntary. The most the mediator can do in the case of a deliberate leak is to apprise the leaking party of the danger of leaks and perhaps elicit a promise that the error will not be repeated.

The mediator must also persuade the other party to refrain from responding in kind, to overlook the leak, and to return to the mediation without rancor or animosity. This prescription may be a hard pill for the victim to swallow, but it is the only way to avoid further damage to the mediation.

Where Mediator Is Misquoted

The same admonition must be issued to the mediator who is misquoted by the media. Certainly the mediator has a right to be irate, but pursuing the matter with media or seeking to reprimand media representatives will bring little satisfaction. Perhaps the mediator can persuade the media of the disservice it does to the parties and the community by publicizing partisan viewpoints or airing other leaks. If such an approach is unproductive, the better course is to ignore the overzealous media and return to the mediation with awareness of the media's propensity to capitalize on what is released to them in the future.

On occasion the mediator's advice to ignore the leak and respect the media ban is ignored by an irate party insisting on getting its licks in with the media. The mediator can then do little more than watch the parties trade proposals and perhaps insults in the media. At some point the mediator must consider advising the parties that the mediation has effectively ended, and that there is no point to continuing it unless both parties agree to return and to discontinue the public warfare. Such a threat of withdrawal may bring a positive response from parties unwilling to lose the mediator. The mediator must hope they will recognize that their media exchanges are even less productive than the mediation.

When a Party Walks Out

The mediator needs two parties to function. If one opts to withdraw from the mediation, the mediator's role has come to an end. Yet the mediator must be prepared to deal with the threat of a walkout and with the act itself if it does occur. Clearly that prospect is not a pleasant one, and one can be sure that the party prepared to depart is not happy with the progress of the mediation, and probably not happy with the mediator. The threat of departure generally comes at a particularly tense stage of the mediation, is motivated by a particularly strong sense of frustration, and is not an empty gesture for the benefit (or pain) of the other side.

The mediator obviously lacks authority to stop the departure. At best, if alerted to the prospect early enough, the mediator may be able to talk the rebelling party out of its proposed action. If the mediator is the cause of the dissatisfaction, the obvious course for the mediator is to offer to withdraw from the case and for the parties to select a replacement. But if the cause of the unrest is something else, the mediator must explain the risks of a departure. One of these is that the mediator will announce to the media that the party has quit the process. Not only does this party provide media fodder for the other side, which can garner much favorable publicity from its willingness to continue while its adversary has left; it also creates a problem of return for the departing party. Since the parties must ultimately reach accord, the departed party at some point must resume negotiations.

Impact of Departure

If these entreaties and threats do not work and the party still insists on departing, the mediator must decide whether to declare the mediation at an end or to provide an opportunity for the departing party to return. If the mediator senses that the departure is a matter of pique, it might be desirable to declare a recess in the mediation, with the acquiescence of the departing party. The mediator could meet with both spokespersons and advise them that the mediation has not been terminated and the departure is being treated as temporary. If unwilling to provide the remaining party with ammunition to use against the departing party, the mediator might simply advise the remaining side that there is to be a temporary break in the proceedings, not volunteering but not denying that the other party is refusing to participate. The mediator can explain the haitus to the press as a temporary recess, as an opportunity for the parties to rethink their positions, as a time for securing authorization for further movement, or as a period for research into prevailing practices.

If the mediator believes that a later reopening of the mediation is not possible, the procedure for avoiding exploitation of that departure by the other side might be to announce to both and perhaps to the media that the parties have agreed to end the mediation, and will jointly determine whether to resume direct negotiations or move to fact finding after a brief respite. Although such an announcement might be viewed as less than candid, there is nothing to be gained by announcing that the parties are no longer communicating. And since it is inevitable that relations will be resumed at some point, the euphemisms are not entirely inaccurate. The role of the mediator is to encourage the parties to come together, not to issue pronouncements underscoring their intransigence. The wording of the mediator's announcement, if it is hopeful enough, may provide the departed party with the face saver it needs to come back into the negotiations or even back into the mediation process. Mediators who are still acceptable usually tell the parties they will stand ready to assist them to resume the mediation or to make arrangements to use the services of another mediator or a fact finder.

Language Block

The process of contract negotiation involves the resolution of two sets of disputes on each issue. The first is agreement on the concepts involved in a particular provision. The second is agreement on the language that is to be included in the parties' agreement. In many cases the problems are combined, with the parties negotiating the concept within the framework of carefully drafted contract proposals and counterproposals. Agreement is frequently attained on the basis of such proposals. But at other times the parties are unable to agree to the specific wording, although they may agree upon the concept behind the differing language versions. Negotiations between the parties may dwell upon concepts with no attention paid to specific wording; on the other hand, the parties may focus on language differences without really coming to grips with the underlying concept. In either case the mediator may be called upon to translate concept into specific contract language.

Such an undertaking has its personal risks for the mediator. There is the risk of coming up with wording that is viewed as overly favorable to one side. There is the risk of coming up with language which does not solve the parties' disagreement, or even triggers further disagreement between them. Mediators are not necessarily gifted or skilled draftsmen of contract language. They often lack experience in this area, and may be more adept at jotting down conceptual language that is acceptable to the mediating parties than in drafting specific contract language that is precise enough to deter grievances over its interpretation. The mediator may rely too heavily on grievance stimulating words such as reasonableness, equality, fair judgment, and the like. Although the mediator may secure the agreement of the negotiators on such language, appreciation of the effort may be short lived if the terminology gives rise to many grievance and arbitration cases. To avoid the problems that may result, the mediator faced with this responsibility would do well to secure the assistance of a team member from each party, preferably individuals with prior language experience so that they can share their expertise as well as the onus for the language finally agreed upon.

Assessing Priorities Incorrectly

Issues on a bargaining table are confusing, contradictory, complicated, and frequently indecipherable to an outsider. One of the putative skills of the mediator is that of culling out those few issues that both parties are most concerned about and focusing the attention of the two teams on them. These are the priority issues. The other issues fall into different categories but are of less concern and not important enough, win or lose, to interfere with the parties' reaching a settlement. In theory, agreement on the priority issues will restore harmony to the parties' relationship and end the dispute, with the ancillary issues "falling into place."

Identifying Priorities

Mediators vary in their technique for selecting the priorities and in determining which to pursue. A top priority for the union, maintenance of full health insurance, for example, may seem of little importance to the employer who is willing to allocate agreed-on new money as the union prefers.

Because the union gives the issue a high priority, which might hold up a settlement, it takes on significance for the employer as well. The employer may be more concerned about a contract clause that restricts the right to subcontract work, while employees who have been working substantial weekly overtime for the past year may pay little heed to that issue. Yet it comes into the union's focus because it is a high management priority.

The mediator is generally able to recognize the high-priority issues from prior experience in similar relationships, from the statements of the teams about their respective proposals, and from the reactions to those proposals.

Mediators are of two schools in determining priorities. The more aggressive, or "deal maker," mediators seek a prompt identification of priorities in their initial contacts with parties. The more conservative mediators, the orchestrators, avoid pushing the parties to identify their priorities and instead seek to glean this information from the statements made and positions taken by the teams in joint or separate sessions.

Mediators who seek to identify priorities quickly and those who let the list take shape from the exchanges both run the risk of misassessing priorities. This may happen in several ways. First, a team may be unwilling to reveal a priority to the mediator for fear that it may be leaked to the other side. Perhaps the union seeks the removal of a cap on overtime or some other improvement but is downplaying it for fear that emphasizing it will bring resistance. The team strategy may be to work for a broader contract change that would automatically achieve its narrower goal.

Second, the mediator may evaluate the importance of an item on the basis of erroneous or incomplete information. For example, the union may confide that the employer is contemplating cutbacks but must delay the notification date in order to protect previously committed funding. In fact, the employer has no such need. Acceptance of the union's assessment will give the mediator an incorrect picture of the employer's priorities.

Third, a priority list may change. The union at the outset may give top priority to reduction-in-force language. Later it discovers that the employer is not laying off but rather contemplating recruiting. Perhaps the union is told the intent to recruit in confidence and keeps its RIF demand on the table for the sake of appearance. The mediator may then wrongly assume that it is still a top priority.

The mediator must remain alert to the accuracy of the priority list, and must be attuned to changes of priorities and to the possibility that a team is using its priority list as a red herring to deceive the mediator and the other team.

By focusing on the important items, the mediator can contribute greatly to the process and perhaps hasten a settlement. An incorrect assessment of priorities, on the other hand, can impede the settlement process. In one case with which the author is familiar, the mediator, after being informed of the union's primary objectives, asked the union for its assessment of the employer's goals and was told that money was the only problem, with the employer adamant on a 4-percent increase. Upon meeting with the employer's team, the mediator was told that management's aims were to limit the increase in compensation to 4½ percent and to achieve "changes in three or four contract provisions."

The mediator went to work on the union's objectives and the money question and in a series of mediation sessions resolved all but the money question. Then in the final session that was settled, and the mediator announced settlement. At this juncture the employer's representative simply asked "When are we going to do those three or four contract changes that are our priorities?"

This case illustrates the danger of becoming swept up in one side's list of priorities and ignoring those that a quiet or timid team may present less forcefully. It also shows the hazard in relying on only one side's assessment of priorities and not making a periodic assessment of the status of *all* pending issues. It is crucial that the mediator carefully check the open issues from time to time during the mediation—and certainly before announcing settlement.

Incomplete Deliveries

The mediator must also be sensitive to the forcefulness of his or her own personality. In seeking to achieve agreement on the critical matters in dispute, the mediator may mislead a team as to the status of an item. An aside such as "I can get that for you" makes it as good as won in the perception of the team. The mediator who makes such a statement had better be sure the item in question can be delivered. Too many shattered mediators return with, "I'm sorry. I really thought that was what they meant," or "I didn't think they would care about that," or "You'll have to give up the following first."

Summary

There are times when the relationship between the parties falters because of a perception on the part of one or both parties that the absence of movement is attributable to the action—or inaction—of the mediator. There may be a challenge to the mediator's impartiality, or a claim that a message was improperly transmitted, or a claim that one of the parties or the mediator made an unauthorized statement to the media. The mediator may also be blamed for the parties' inability to agree on language, or for a number of other difficulties. What these situations all have in common is that they put pressure upon the mediator and make it doubtful whether he can continue to be part of the process.

No mediator is indispensable. A mediator can readily be replaced, and should not continue when his presence is a source of conflict rather than a means to its elimination. In such cases the mediator should seek to alleviate the parties' concerns and put them back on the road to settlement. But if the questions concerning the mediator's role cannot be met to the parties' joint satisfaction, the proper course of conduct is for the mediator to withdraw from the case. Despite their misgivings, the most likely response from the parties will be a request that the mediator continue in the case and a willingness to accept proposals made by the mediator to resume movement toward settlement.

15
ENDING THE MEDIATION

Regardless of how long the mediation lasts, whether it be hours, days, or weeks; regardless of the animosities and challenges and crises that mark the process; and regardless of the standing of the mediator in the eyes of the parties, the mediation must inevitably come to a close. That end may be a successful resolution of the conflict and agreement on the terms of a new collective bargaining agreement. It may also be an acrimonious parting of the ways without agreement and with the prospect of continuing hostility until the inevitable agreement is reached.

A mediation in which the parties work toward a settlement in a spirit of cooperation and compromise may not really need the participation of the mediator to bring the final settlement. The rapport between the parties may be sufficient. But often there will be stumbling blocks in the last sessions of even the most harmonious of mediations. The services of the mediator may then be needed to bring the mediation to a close, or at least to remove the impediments to the parties reaching their own agreement.

The role of the mediator in these final steps of the mediation must be performed with care and sensitivity.

Deadlocks Over Minor Issues

It is not unusual for even the most cooperative parties to reach a deadlock over some issue toward the end of the mediation. When the more crucial and substantive issues have been resolved and it appears that only trivial issues remain, the seemingly unimportant issues take on a life of their own. The last remaining issue, no matter how insignificant it may have been before, becomes the biggest issue in the mediation. A party that thinks it has the other side on the run may take a harsh stance on a remaining issue in the belief that the other side will be unable to resist. Likewise, the party that is on the defensive, feeling that it may have given away too much or too soon, may stiffen its resistance in a face-saving gesture in order to salvage as much as possible. Regardless of the motivation, the parties often will work themselves into a deadlock over some of the final issues of the mediation.

When faced with such a deadlock, the mediator would do well to recite to the parties the consequences of their inflexibility. This can be done together or separately. A joint session makes sense when the mediator perceives that both parties can move to a compromise position. Separate sessions may be preferable when the mediator is seeking to get one of the parties to move toward an accommodation the other party has already made. In these sessions, whether joint or separate, the mediator should emphasize the cost the parties are attaching to the issue in terms of what it might do to the rest of their negotiations, the risk they run of destroying the settlement on the more substantial issues, and the consequences of deadlock continuing to strike and thereafter. Frequently when what had been a minor issue escalates to a major issue toward the end of the mediation, the parties lose perspective. They tend to attach undue importance to the issue, and may lose sight of the fact that a refusal to settle because of the dispute on a minor issue will leave the negotiators looking petulant or foolish in the eyes of the community.

There are several ways in which the mediator may try to help the parties. One approach is to try to bring the parties to settlement on the particular stumbling block. Another is to attempt to structure a package comprising a number of outstanding issues so that neither party will perceive a change of position on the deadlocked issue as a loss. Sometimes it may even be possible to go back into issues that have already been tentatively agreed to in order to bring forward something for reconsideration to make the package of the remaining issues more attractive.

There are a number of techniques that might be utilized to break the deadlock. There may be an offer of a "sweetener," a change in the timing of benefits, or a rewriting of disputed language. If the mediator senses that settlement is impeded only by a fear that the two sides might be settling too soon even though all other elements are in place, encouraging the offer of a sweetener may be enough to persuade the reluctant party into agreement, or at a minimum to induce a counterproposal that might prove acceptable. The mediator might also propose a restructuring of the time schedule, delaying introduction of a controversial item, making it a subject of a later contract reopener, or converting percentages to fixed dollar figures.

Sometimes conflicts over terminology can be resolved by the mediator's substitution of new language for what the parties have been fighting over. "Fuzzy" words such as "every reasonable effort shall be made" may be welcomed by the parties to resolve a deadlock over wording. Even though the parties are aware that vague terms may open the door to grievances during the life of the contract, they may prefer that possibility to continued conflict over more precise language.

The Team Spoiler

The mediator may sense that the resistance to movement and the rejection of possible settlement packages is not team-wide. If there is evidence of a "spoiler" in one or both of the teams, it may be prudent to discuss the package proposals privately with the spokespersons. In that way it may be possible to bring the spokespersons into agreement on a final package and have them jointly announce it as a fait accompli.

If one or both spokespersons are the spoilers, it may be wiser for the mediator to attempt to bypass them by meeting with the more compliant teams. In one mediation the union spokesperson was a depressed and reputedly friendless woman whose sole social outlet and place in the sun was the negotiations. She presumably viewed the termination of the mediation as a sentence to loneliness and stubbornly resisted efforts to close out the case. At a team meeting I spoke to her within earshot of the team about the good faith of the proposed employer package. When she rejected it, a team member said, "Let us caucus," and after several minutes the spokesperson announced the team's acceptance of the proposal.

Selfish motives may also cause team members to impede efforts to reach final settlement. They may believe that excessive resistance to the other side's offers will prove their loyalty and that such loyalty will be rewarded with better positions within their respective establishments. Fortunately, the higher-ups in management and labor are wary of those who impede the dispute settlement process for personal gain.

The mediator generally should turn to the spokespersons rather than to team members for an objective view of the situation. they are more likely to place a high priority on settlement, and are more likely to provide the best guidance to the mediator. In my experience, leveling with the spokespersons in seeking to find the most palatable and least abrasive way out of a dilemma will provide insights and approaches that the mediator alone would never have thought of. The spokespersons have a far better sense of what it will take to work things out, and I have found that their perceptions are not that far apart. Once such a potent team has worked out an acceptable end result, or even an acceptable scenario for reaching such a result, it can determine the appropriate role for the mediator, whether to reduce tensions, to serve as the villain, or to push the parties along a secretly predetermined route. For the mediator, it is far more important to maintain the respect and acceptance of the spokespersons than to be viewed as a hero by the members of one of the teams.

Breaking the Mediation

If the mediator is unable to break the deadlock with or without the help of the spokespersons, it is appropriate to face the reality that the mediation may be dead. Perhaps the stronger party will not provide the face saver that is needed to bring the loser to accommodation. Perhaps the losing party is holding firm on the final issue in the hope that the other side will permit it to salvage something. Perhaps the spokespersons, victims of their teams or unwilling to cooperate with each other, are at fault. Or perhaps the mediator is at fault for not taking advantage of the right opening at the right time, or for failing to come up with a substitute plan or alternative that the parties could turn to as a way out of their dilemma. The source of the fault does not matter and really should not be identified, for at this stage fault-finding brings no forward movement but only recrimination and frustration. The mediation must be considered dead, at least for the moment. Naturally the mediator should apply the lessons of the preceding chapter and, while talking as though the process were dead, nonetheless should try to persuade the parties to leave the door open to a later resumption of the process.

When confronted with a joint intention to cut off talks, I have sought to arrange a private meeting with the spokespersons away from the battle scene. On one occasion when the issue was joined at 2 A.M., I proposed that the spokespersons and I meet for a bite at a nearby restaurant. Sometimes merely taking a ride or going to a cocktail lounge for a drink provides a sufficient change of setting to encourage a fresh look at the situation. It may not alter the determination to abandon mediation, but it gives the mediator an opportunity to suggest changes in the manner of closing things down. There may be proposals by the mediator for a break to reassess positions, or that the parties seek greater authority from their principals in order to permit movement into areas as yet unexplored. But these proposals for leaving the door open may be rebuffed. The mediator may be faced with the hard reality that a continuation of the process is not of interest to the parties.

At the juncture the choice may be between silent withdrawal and going down with flags flying. It may be tempting to point to the failure of the parties to respond positively to the problem solving proposals of the mediator. This approach will solve no problems, and will only invite recriminations by the parties for errors that the mediator is thought to have made. A more constructive approach is to bring the parties together and explain that, since there appears to be no prospect of further movement, the mediator believes that it would be better to withdraw than to continue wasting both parties' time and money. Such an announcement should be accompanied by private encouragement for the parties to get together at some time in the future to discuss the status of their relationship. To this proposal the mediator might also disclaim any intention to announce a permanent end to the mediation, leaving the parties free to reopen the process when they have cooled down, when they have reconsidered their proposals, or when they have additional authority to move into areas not previously explored.

Even after all these exchanges have taken place and everyone recognizes that the mediation is over, the persistent mediator may not be through. More than one failed mediation has been saved by a last-minute intervention by the mediator. On one occasion I was in my car driving away when I thought of a repackaging that might work and raced back to share it with the spokespersons. A phone call the next day may salvage the matter also. The mediator should not give up merely because the parties have. The right prescription, even though it comes late in the game, may serve to get the process grinding forward again.

Alternatives to Mediation

If it is clear that mediation services are no longer wanted, the mediator might propose that the parties try some other form of dispute settlement. Sometimes the next step following a failed mediation is prescribed by statute, or by the parties' own contract. The next step is usually fact finding, and beyond that there may be a commitment by statute or agreement to go to arbitration.

In a typical fact finding, the neutral hears evidence concerning the items in dispute and then makes nonbinding recommendations for the resolution of the conflict. If the failure of the mediation is not laid at the feet of the mediator, the parties may desire that the mediator assume the mantle of fact finder as well. It is more likely, however, that they will wish to have a fresh face fulfilling that role.

Another choice might be arbitration, either conventional arbitration or final-offer selection, in which each of the parties places a final package before the arbitrator, who then chooses one of the two proposals.

The mediator might make other suggestions to the parties, including continuation of the present agreement for another year or the issuance of a recommended settlement of the issues in dispute. Such an unsolicited offer of recommendations is unlikely to be accepted by both parties; the side that feels it is in the weaker position might endorse the idea, but the other side probably would not. Actually, the threat of recommendations is more effective than their issuance, and may be sufficient to lure the parties back to the bargaining table. For the mediator to make recommendations is likely to exacerbate the situation by giving the weaker party new ammunition with which to attack the unreasonableness of the other side, thus reducing the likelihood that it will accept the terms offered by the other side.

Nonetheless, the mediator on occasion may feel that unsolicited recommendations for settlement are warranted. Such recommendations may be a valuable device for heading off a threatened strike, as, for example, where the mediator has a better feel for the issues than the parties and a sense that a certain formula will fly even if not endorsed by or cleared in advance with the parties. This might be so where there is a middle ground between the parties' positions that had not been explored in the earlier discussions for resolving the dispute. Recommendations, if made, should be proposed as a guide for the parties' further discussions.

Forcing the Parties On

If the parties express a desire to give the mediation a last try, and if the mediator believes that an intense effort may be fruitful, it may make sense to force the parties on by means of a marathon mediation session. It is not uncommon for the mediator to advise the parties that a session will continue indefinitely without interruption. This is particularly the case when good progress is being made or when a deadline is at hand. To attempt to hold a marathon session when the parties are in agreement that the mediation should cease is obviously inadvisable; the parties would refuse to attend the session or walk out. But if the parties are willing, and if the mediator senses that one of them has room for movement, or that both are holding back more than they should at so late a stage of the mediation, a marathon mediation session may have value.

Certainly there is drama to an all-night meeting, and team members attach importance to such a meeting. The parties must, however, experience the pressure of a meaningful deadline. In the private sector, the contract expiration date may be a meaningful deadline if the union has a policy of no contract, no work. In the public sector, however, something more normally is needed. A statement by the mediator that further meetings are not possible because of a crowded calendar may be sufficient to jolt the teams into recognizing that the end is at hand. Such a statement will be more credible if the mediator is from out of town and particularly if the mediator has a reputation of leaving at the announced departure time. Even the most relaxed team members are likely to realize that a failure to settle by the mediator's departure time will end the mediation and force them to resort to some other form of dispute settlement, such as fact finding.

A marathon session should be proposed by the mediator only if there is a prospect that wearing down one or both parties will bring about movement toward settlement. The mediator who embarks upon such a session must be certain that he possesses the stamina to outlast the advocates. If the mediator has calculated correctly, an all-night session may well provide satisfying results. There is always a risk that a reluctant party will reconsider any concessions made during a marathon session and withdraw them. The mediator therefore should have reason to believe the parties will stand by any commitments they may make.

If the mediator senses during a marathon session that one of the teams is faltering and ready to quit, it is usually possible to avoid a walkout by pointing out that the teams are close to settlement and that the public will blame the party walking out for the breakdown. In an exceptional case the mediator may agree to stay on beyond the announced departure time, but should do this only if there is persuasive evidence that a settlement is imminent. Such evidence may also justify a deadline postponement, or an offer to return at a later date. The mediator's goal is to secure an agreement, not to pull out of the process. Declarations of firm intention to leave at a stated time are calculated to stimulate the necessary moves to achieve a settlement; if such a declaration does produce meaningful negotiations, the mediator should, if possible, remain available to the end.

The Mediator's Proposal

A device that can be employed in connection with a marathon session or separately is the "mediator's proposal." The mediator's proposal—quite different from unsolicited recommendations that the mediator might make in a last-ditch effort to prevent the parties from terminating the mediation—is a prearranged recommendation for settlement that the spokespersons know about and are committed to sell to their teams or to their principals. It is in essence an informed fact-finding recommendation.

Use of the mediator's proposal may be appropriate when the spokespersons have let it be known that they can reach agreement but are having problems with their teams. The mediator asks them to persuade their teams to request, or at least acquiesce in, a proposal from the mediator for settlement of all remaining issues. The mediator then proposes as a basis for settlement the terms the spokespersons have indicated are acceptable to them. It is understood that the proposal, covering all outstanding issues, must be accepted as a total package or not at all, and that neither party has the option of selecting some elements while rejecting others.

The mediator's proposal has both the advantage and the disadvantage of finality. It brings the mediation to an end if it is accepted as the final settlement, but it probably will end the participation of the mediator if it is rejected. The mediator may, of course, agree to continue in the case if the parties so request, but many would contend that the mediator could do so only with diminished credibility.

The Inevitable Settlement

Employers and unions in both the private sector and the public sector must live with each other, and must ultimately reach agreement on wages, hours, and the working conditions that will guide their living together. Settlement may not come in the presence of the mediator or even during the mediation sessions. It may come long after the mediator has withdrawn from the case, after a strike or lockout or following an interest arbitration, or as a result of a secret understanding between the principals without the participation of the mediator and perhaps even their spokespersons. Fortunately for mediators and for the public, mediation is successful in resolving disputes in which it is invoked. Far fewer settlements occur following a failure of mediation.

Accordingly, the mediator can generally look forward to the happy culmination of the mediation effort in a joint agreement resolving the parties' dispute. This is not to say that both parties will be happy with the outcome. Perhaps both will seem a little disappointed, in which case the mediator can conclude that the settlement, while perhaps only tolerable, is probably a fair one. If one of the parties is overjoyed and the other morose, the mediator ought not to add to the feeling of persecution of the losing party but rather should warn the elated party of the emotional damage it may be doing to the other side. Sometimes a defeat can be minimized by having the weaker party make the final offer and the stronger party accept it. Then the party that has failed to bring home the bacon can at least proclaim that the other side "agreed to our final proposal," which sounds a lot better than, "We had to cave in and take what they offered."

In many cases where the settlement agreement has to be ratified by the union rank and file, the mediator, with an eye on the politics of ratification, may try to keep the employer from making the final offer, working instead to find out what the proffered terms will be and then advising the union to propose them to the employer. The employer then appears to be the one that is "caving in." This frequently has great appeal when a questionable settlement comes up for ratification. Many mediators insist that the spokesperson make the final offer for fear that if relayed by the mediator it will suggest further bargaining is possible. This may indeed spell the difference between membership acceptance and rejection of the settlement.

What should the mediator do when the parties have reached agreement? My practice is to bring the two teams together and announce that an agreement has been reached. I then list the elements of the final package so all will know that what is in the package is what they thought they were agreeing to. Some mediators assist the parties in drafting language to express agreements in principle or agreements based on broad concepts. I do not follow this practice, feeling that the ministerial duty of writing the agreement should be handled by the representatives of the parties or their attorneys. They, rather than the mediator, should be held responsible for later questions of contract interpretation or applicaton. Moreover, drafting is best done away from the glare of the joint proceedings and the scrutiny of the team members.

Complaints

The difficulty of reviewing the terms of the settlement sometimes is compounded by a claim that one or more elements was not in fact agreed upon. Such a claim usually does not come from the spokespersons but rather from a disgruntled team member harboring resentment that the team did not get all it sought on one or more particular issues. Nonetheless, despite the risk that rancor might surface during a review of the settlement terms, it is important to make sure that the teams, which may have been hearing the elements of the mediation in separate sessions through a series of relayed messages, do in fact agree on the terms of settlement. Misunderstandings do occur, and they must be aired and resolved before the final language is put to paper.

Reading the Terms

It is not uncommon for something to come to light during the final reading of the terms that had been overlooked or mistakenly dealt with.

Surprisingly, such problems usually are readily resolved, since neither party at that stage is willing to let a relatively insignificant issue spoil the more important agreement on the big issues. It may be possible to bend with the situation and make a concession on the issue in question, but that approach works only once. Repeated use encourages multiple reopening of items the parties thought had been closed.

Sometimes, in lieu of a full statement of the terms, the parties will ask the mediator to write up an agreement containing the major points of the settlement. This writing provides a document that the parties can sign to indicate a commitment to the settlement.

Ratification

Once the settlement announcement has been completed, and perhaps has been toasted with a bottle of champagne supplied by the mediator, the next step is ratification. Ratification is rarely a problem on the employer side. The authorization of the management team is usually so explicit that the team is unlikely to have exceeded it, and what it has agreed to is therefore seldom rejected. Ratification is further assured by the centralization of management and the ease of communication by telephone or conference during the mediation to make sure that the team acts within its authority, or to secure authority beyond previous bounds if the case so requires.

On the union side the issue of ratification is more troublesome. It is difficult to keep the membership alert to the details of the progress of negotiations and mediation. It is also difficult to consult the membership during the mediation to adjust positions and to increase the negotiators' authority. The membership customarily permits the leadership or the negotiating team to go as far as it deems necessary to settle, retaining the right to accept or reject the settlement when it comes before the membership for ratification. The ratification process is complicated by the fact that the union is likely to have proclaimed its goals publicly, leading the membership to believe that what was demanded would in fact be attained. Thus the union that does not bring home all that it set out to achieve may be subject to criticism in the ratification meeting, particularly if there is a rival organization in the picture.

As a result of these pressures, ratification is not so routine a matter for the union as it is for the employer. Settlements sometimes are rejected; ratifications do fail; and mediation settlements as a consequence do fall apart.

Mediators differ as to the role they should play in these situations. Some will readily go to a ratification meeting to explain the nature of the settlement, much as they would go to the teams directly. Others refrain from speaking to either union or management groups outside the mediation. My feeling is that the teams are there in a representative capacity and that it is their responsibility and not that of the mediator to sell the settlement. It is not the responsibility of the mediator to do their work at the ratification meeting.

Mediators also differ as to their proper role when there is a rejection of a settlement by the union membership. Some recall the parties and recommend that the mediation be reopened. Others take the position that they have given the dispute their best shot and that it is to the parties' advantage to negotiate thereafter on their own or to secure the services of a different mediator.

The parties may jointly request the return of the same mediator, particularly if their relationship was satisfactory and their intentions were the same. Frequently the employer will be unwilling to enhance the package, but it may be willing to recast the package within the same dollar limit to make it more acceptable to the union membership. The mediator who has been a party to the evolution of the original package may indeed be the best person to help the parties redo the package. A mediator who had made a mediator's proposal that he thought represented the best possible settlement might, however, be reluctant to return to the mediation.

Summary

The end of the mediation process is filled with a great number of pitfalls. The parties may agree to dismiss the mediator and break off the mediation. The mediator may withdraw, expressing the view that nothing more can be accomplished through mediation. The end may come in a long and tortured session at which the mediator tries to bring about the best possible settlement. The mediator may make recommendations, either at the parties' request or over their objections. The most desirable climax is a settlement followed by ratification by the principals on both sides.

Whatever the final steps of the process entail, the mediator continues to have an important role in shaping the settlement, and in making sure that it holds together through these final stages. A successful conclusion gives the mediator the satisfaction of having helped the parties. It is important to remember, however, that the mediator did not achieve the settlement. The parties did. The mediator may have helped, but it was the parties' process and *their* successful mediation.

16
CONCLUSIONS

The process of mediation is captivating. It brings together two opposing parties, frequently antagonistic and hostile in their relationship; interposes a third party between them, often of their mutual selection; and creates thereby the expectation that the three forces will be able to achieve an agreement when the two parties could not. The addition of the third party to the traditional two-party system increases the complexity of the structure but makes it more effective.

Even the participants in the process often are astonished that it actually works. Much is dependent on the desire of the parties to reach agreement, on their willingness to compromise, and on the skill of the mediator in exploiting that willingness. But it is important to recognize and remember that it is the mixture of elements rather than any individual factor or participant that makes the process work.

Caveats for the Mediators

The public perception of the process is that the mediator enters the fray like a knight in shining armor, and through magical incantations forces the parties to settlement. Any one who has sat through the long, grueling hours or days of a mediation, waiting for responses, struggling to secure the agreement of one side and then the other to a change of a word or two in a proposal, recognizes that the public perception is inaccurate. The mediator runs the greatest risk of falling under the spell of public perception. The least experienced mediators, those new to the field, tend to take personal credit for the settlements. After all, the mediator enters a dispute in a climate of disagreement and hostility. After what seems an endless series of prods and probes to get the parties to move to what the mediator senses to be a rational middle ground, there is agreement probably close to what the mediator thought would be the outcome. Wouldn't the sessions have ended in failure without the mediator's entreaties and threats? Didn't the parties express appreciation for the result when all was finished?

It is easy for mediators to delude themselves into believing that it is they who achieve the settlements. Since settlement is inevitable in labor-management contract negotiations, despite prolonged periods of rancor and possibly strikes and lockouts, even a mediator who was thrown out of a case by the parties could claim a role in bringing them back together and perhaps even take credit for the eventual settlement. The public may perceive a settlement as a feather in the mediator's cap, but mediators generally content themselves with the satisfaction that comes when the parties express thanks "for all you've done to bring us together."

Mediators must also balance that satisfaction against the feelings of guilt they experience when the mediation fails. Certainly they assume much of the blame when settlement is not achieved. The mediator who follows the parties out of the meeting place when an unsuccessful mediation ends engages in intensive soul searching as to what went wrong. What should have been done differently? Should that last proposal have been recast with a different emphasis? Should the reluctant party have been pushed to offer just a little bit more? Should there have been a threat to go public when the parties refused to stay any longer? The mediator is lonely enough when he leaves the scene without a settlement. It is only natural that there should be a lot of second guessing over what might have been done to pull a settlement out of a deadlock.

In these self-flagellations the mediator too often totally ignores what the parties did to block the mediator's conscientious efforts to move them toward settlement, what they could have done to help reach the settlement, and whether either or both ever intended to even try for a settlement. Instead the mediator focuses on what he did or might have done as though he were dealing with inanimate parties whose participation came only in response to the initiatives of the mediator.

The Parties' Role

It takes many mediations, with a suitable blend of successes and failures, for the new mediator to recognize that it is the parties rather than the neutral who are the prime decision makers controlling the outcome of their mediation. It is, in final analysis, their process, and they must bear the consequences, good or bad, of their involvement. Mediators who assist them in their efforts ultimately come to accept the fact after many cases that the neutral's role is far less crucial and indeed that they may be manipulated far more often than they manipulate the parties. The mediators in some instances may bear responsibility for a tactical change or two, but it is the parties who are the strategists and do most of the pulling of strings. Whatever the result of the mediation, it is attributable more to their actions than to the endeavors of the transient intervenor.

Once a mediator is able to disclaim credit for success, it becomes easier to be objective about the failures, and to recognize that the mediator is not personally accountable for the failure or the refusal of the parties to overcome their hostility and reach agreement. After years of mediation, the neutral may come to realize that the role of facilitator could have been performed better in settlements, and that no one could have done more to deter the breakdown in nonsettlements.

Parties bent upon settlement will usually achieve it even if the mediator has blundered throughout the case. If the mediator did not meet their expectations, or if they believe that the mediator impeded or delayed their efforts to reach agreement, or missed the messages or cues they provided, they will select a different mediator in their next dispute. By the same token, if the mediation collapsed and there was a bitter strike before the parties finally settled, the parties may nevertheless employ the same mediator in their next impasse if they believe that he kept things from becoming worse, or that they might have avoided a strike by following the mediator's suggestions. Or they may recommend that mediator's services to other parties faced with a comparable dispute. Such endorsements do wonders for the mediator's fragile ego.

Learning From Errors

Mediators who are able to separate their performance from the end result of the mediation begin to learn from their errors and become better mediators. They become more concerned about what they could have done better in all cases, even those that settled. Not only is experience the best teacher; for most mediators it is the only teacher. Except for those fortunate enough to have entered the field following training provided by the FMCS or some of the state agencies, there are minimal opportunities for the mediator who wishes to upgrade skills. Training opportunities are provided for arbitrators through the facilities and publications of the American Arbitration Association and the National Academy of Arbitrators. The perhaps even more pressing need to make such facilities available to mediators has been largely ignored. The Society of Professionals in Dispute Resolution is an example of an organization that has shifted its emphasis to meet the need—moving from emphasis on labor arbitration to concentrate on mediation of all types.

Training Needs

Some of the old-time mediators in the private sector contend that mediators are born and not made—that there are innate qualities that make up a successful mediator, that the necessary skills cannot be taught, and that education is far less relevant for mediators than experience and more experience. Without debating the issue of heredity v. environment which the old timers' dichotomy suggests, it is clear that giving a classroom course to anyone who claims he wants to become a mediator will not necessarily produce a successful neutral.

The best schooling in mediation comes neither from texts nor from lectures. It comes from doing. Just as the success or failure of a mediator in a particular case is in reality the "success" or "failure" of the parties, so too is the education of the mediator the education provided by the parties. Most of those who become mediators, even those lucky enough to be under the tutelage of federal or state agencies or other mediators, do so only as a result of the energies of the parties who undertake to employ them. These mediators may have an innate ability to deal with people or to calm troubled waters, but their practical skills as mediators are acquired primarily through experience. Many novices try to enter the field but are not selected. Even those who are selected may not survive their first test of battle or gain the confidence of the adversaries that is needed for reemployment. Some new entrants, however, do a credible job in the eyes of the adversaries, are accepted or recommended by them for use in succeeding impasses, and through trial and error survive and become professional mediators.

The greatest problem mediators face in improving their competence is the scarcity of continuing education. Without even considering the issue of whether there should be a training program to increase the number of new mediators, or new amateurs, there should be more than occasional conferences attended by a handful of the "in" mediators. Virtually no continuing education is available for this critical group of our society's dispute settlers.

Some mediators have been successful in attaching themselves to the apron strings of more experienced mediators, thereby acquiring a sounding board which they can use to gain information about their performance or about what they should have done. A few even are able, as I was in my first case, to take a break in the mediation proceedings and appeal by telephone to their mentor to ask what to do next. But most of the newer mediators do not enjoy that luxury. They acquire professionalism by experience and plain old trial and error. They receive no assessment from the parties who have been dealing with them as to what they did that was good and what they did that was bad. They never get an opportunity to replay the mediation in front of a more experienced mediator and find out how they could have better handled a particular problem. The real world of mediation does not provide for after-the-fact exchanges between client and mediator. And there is no organized institution to provide the neophyte with needed access to the experienced mediator.

If mediation is to gain in acceptance, if the parties are to have faith in the ability of their mediators, and if new mediators are rapidly to acquire the competence that is needed to guarantee their continued usefulness, a comprehensive program of continuing education coupled with some form of "hot line" to experienced mediators should be made available.

Mediation is becoming the forum of preference in an ever larger number of communities and states, and in an expanding number of fields. The geographical areas where it is being increasingly used are in many cases not where the experienced private sector mediators are situated and available. Inexperienced mediators are being used continuously. Unless a concerted effort is undertaken by the parties or by the institutions in society that endorse this forum for dispute resolution, faith in the process is likely to be diminished and its use curtailed. Public sector mediation still enjoys a respect that spills over from its reputation in the private sector. More must be done to protect the acceptability of the neutrals and the institution itself.

Refresher courses should be offered by neutral organizations such as state agencies, following the model of the New York Public Employment Relations Board. The American Arbitration Association, the Federal Mediation and Conciliation Service, the Society of Professionals in Dispute Resolution, the Association of Labor Relations Agencies, and regional consortiums of state agencies should expand their efforts at training, opening it to those not members of, or on the rosters of, such organizations. Industrial relations centers at universities should also make such programs available in the form of seminars, courses, written study guides, audio-visual packages, and the like.

Unfortunately, as in the case of continuing education for arbitrators, those who need the training the most often are unwilling to take it—or, worse, are unaware that they need it. They may view "their" settlements as proof of their competence and be content with the frequency of their selection without recognizing the value or need of improving the quality of their performance. They may, perhaps, be past salvaging. But many more mediators who have come to recognize that performance is only tangentially related to case settlement are a fertile market for such undertakings.

Career Opportunities

Mediation has had a good press. The high status increasingly accorded the process, the excitement of the work, the glories of the settlements, and the income of those who have succeeded in it as a career have induced a large number of newcomers to enter. They tend to ignore whether they have the basic attributes that make mediators acceptable to the parties, and not to recognize that a long period of experience-building is required. They tend to ignore the fact that the parties prefer to employ the few experienced mediators and construe the limited availability of the few as evidence of a shortage. They tend to ignore the cyclical nature of the work, which virtually precludes anyone from making a living solely as a mediator except as an agency employee. Additionally, they tend to ignore the provinciality of most clients, who are reluctant to expend large sums of money to bring unknowns from another area, particularly if they are inexperienced. Next time, perhaps, but not for this case. The freedom of choice the parties have in selecting mediators leads them to the busy, established mediators and tends to freeze out the newcomers, however capable.

New entrants into the field do not become mediators merely by declaring themselves to be such. They must be utilized. Although several of the state agencies have made commendable contributions in encouraging new mediators, these agencies are relatively few in number, are not located where much of the new action is, and lack the resources or authority to solve the acceptability problems in the geographical areas where mediators, new or experienced, are scarce.

Success as a mediator is a function of the faith of the parties more than it is the stamina or determination of the neutral. A long period of waiting without work may be the price for trying. And then, even if the mediator is successful and in demand, the seasonal character of the impasses in the public sector means long intervals of famine between short periods of feast.

Perhaps the most prudent method of breaking into the field is by working in a related area that can provide income and sustenance while the new mediator endeavors to establish a reputation with an experienced mediator or through the benevolent efforts of a state designating agency. Among related areas that might be considered are academic teaching, administrative work for a designating or neutral agency, and work as an advocate. Although identification as an advocate may impede acceptability, it has been an accepted and indeed preferred mode of entry into private sector mediation.

Physical Demands Upon the Mediator

Even broad acceptability and frequent utilization may not bring the kind of success that newcomers anticipate when contemplating entry into the field. Perhaps one of the reasons that there are so few full-time privately employed mediators and why they eventually seek ancillary work such as arbitration is the sheer physical demand of the work. Because of the seasonal nature of impasses, work comes to even the busiest mediator in flurries. This means long days of mediating, and sometimes working through the night, with little respite if the mediator is to take more than one case at a time. The stamina needed to spend three or four nights a week in intensive and stressful all-night sessions during the few weeks of the mediating season is probably more grueling than most bodies can take. The gallons of coffee, the tons of junk food, the nights without sleep, and the abundant tensions experienced by the mediator frequently lead even the successful practitioner to look for more relaxed work with more reasonable hours and a more regular schedule.

There is a masochistic streak in mediators who undertake to work with too many parties during the short work season. The result can be a worn out and increasingly ineffective neutral. Yet if new mediators find a demand for their services, and have the stamina to withstand the pressures of intensive work, there are unquestionably great satisfactions to maintain the ego, if not the pocketbook, during the long periods of inactivity.

Mediation in Other Fields

The American experience with mediation up to this point has been almost exclusively in the field of labor-management relations. Accordingly, labor-management mediation serves as the model for other disciplines that seek to use it for their impasses. In recent years the delays and frustrations and cost of traditional resort to the courts have encouraged litigants to look elsewhere, often with judicial encouragement, for a means of resolving their disputes. Mediation has been used with success in landlord-tenant disputes, in disputes over problems of family law, child custody, divorce settlements, and the like, in disputes involving environmental issues, and of course, in international disputes. It is being heralded as a means of solving problems of hazardous waste disposal, consumer disputes, community conflicts, and many other problems. Clearly the labor-management model is not transferable wholesale to these new areas. The newer types of disputes arise out of a different tradition and with different participant needs and goals and with different roles for the mediator.

In the case of labor-management disputes there is a tradition of court deference to the private settlement procedure the parties have negotiated; this is not true of other kinds of disputes. Participants in the newer disputes usually have a tradition of resorting to the courts, have certain statutory rights that they may invoke, and may be unwilling to surrender those rights for the dubious prospects of resolution through mediation. Mediation is not within the accepted framework of their prior relationships. It may have to be "invented" as a new alternative forum for these disputes, and be given the societal blessing that is enjoyed by labor-management mediation.

Labor-management mediation is founded upon an ongoing relationship and a mutual need and commitment to the goal of preserving the relationship. The parties and the mediator recognize the inevitability of having to work together and the general hands-off attitude of the courts in assuring the fulfillment of that goal. In the new areas of dispute there may be no such commitment by all the parties to the survival of their relationship. Indeed, it may be in the interest of one or more of the participants to bring about the severance of a relationship between others. Entry into mediation may well be with the retention of the right to resort to legal enforcement of other rights and to abandon the mediation process that is not giving total satisfaction. Additionally, parties in the newer disputes may float in and out without the total commitment to the process that is present in labor-management mediation.

The role of the mediator in the labor-management field is sufficiently institutionalized that the parties are conditioned to calling on a ready roster of qualified individuals under an arrangement that recognizes the professionalism of the neutral. How the mediator is to be compensated is preestablished as being a responsibility of the parties or the state or both. Compensation is rarely a subject for discussion between the parties or with the mediator. In the newer fields, there is no such tradition. There are few individuals who have experience in the substance of the fields where the disputes arise. Those who do have such experience are often viewed as prejudiced by some of the participants, and as totally unacceptable by the spoilers. Furthermore, the issue of compensation itself becomes a matter of mediation. Neutrals who are on some payroll may be viewed as unacceptable because of their affiliation. Yet without it there is no ready way for them to maintain their income during their involvement as a mediator. Sometimes foundations contribute to preliminary programs, but compensation is not assured in these areas, as it is in the labor-management field. That deficiency impedes mediations, deters would-be mediators, and at the very least injects a new area of dispute not present in labor-management mediation.

The tradition of a triggering call from the two parties to commence the mediation and the work to settlement or breakdown are unique to labor-management mediation. The diversity and numbers of participants in other areas require mediation merely to determine whether there is to be mediation of substantive issues. And the absence of realistic deadlines in most disputes results in longer periods of dispute, lethargic efforts at mediation, and uncertainties for the mediator as to when the case will commence and how long it will last.

The generally accepted notion in labor-management mediation, that the mediator is but a facilitator, with the parties determining whether a settlement is desirable or in the public interest, is likely to be different from that in the new fields, where public interest and concern may be the stimulus for the mediation, and where the mediator may have a commitment to protect the parties from infringing on or violating the public interest. Whereas the mediation of labor-management disputes is recognized as a private process, new areas of dispute tend to have a public interest involvement that creates a different set of standards for the mediator.

The system of mediation is undoubtedly the forum with the widest appeal and greatest potential for helping parties resolve their ever widening range of conflicts. But its transition to these new fields is fraught with difficulty. Even though labor-management neutrals may have many lessons to impart, they are not necessarily the best individuals to serve the parties in these new fields. But they can help. They can encourage expansion of the institution of mediation, and they can help train the advocates as well as the neutrals in the techniques of negotiation and mediation in these newer fields. In this sense the prospect is greater for adapting the successful labor-management model to, than for adopting it in, these newer areas of conflict. The mediation process has become the standard for the resolution of conflict over new contract disputes in the labor-management field. With patience and assistance from labor-management parties and neutrals it may become a useful and indeed even a vital tool in these newer areas of conflict. If it can be nurtured by the advocates in those fields as it has been in the labor-management field, it may become a more universal standard for resolving societal disputes. Mediators may be able to share the skills they have acquired in the labor-management arena with mediators in other fields of conflict. That it is their obligation to do so, as beneficiaries of the labor-management system and as members of a society overly bent on conflict, is beyond dispute.

APPENDIX

Code of Professional Conduct For Labor Mediators

Adopted Jointly by the Federal Mediation
and Conciliation Service and the Several
State Agencies Represented by the Association
of Labor Mediation Agencies

Preamble

The practice of mediation is a profession with ethical responsibilities and duties. Those who engage in the practice of mediation must be dedicated to the principles of free and responsible collective bargaining. They must be aware that their duties and obligations relate to the parties who engage in collective bargaining, to every other mediator, to the agencies which administer the practice of mediation, and to the general public.

Recognition is given to the varying statutory duties and responsibilities of the city, state and federal agencies. This code, however, is not intended in any way to define or adjust any of these duties and responsibilities nor is it intended to define when and in what situations mediators from more than one agency should participate. It is, rather, a personal code relating to the conduct of the individual mediator.

This code is intended to establish principles applicable to all professional mediators employed by city, state or federal agencies or to mediators privately retained by parties.

1. The Responsibility of the Mediator to the Parties

The primary responsibility for the resolution of a labor dispute rests upon the parties themselves. The mediator at all times should recognize that the agreements reached in collective bargaining are voluntarily made by the parties. It is the mediator's responsibility to assist the parties in reaching a settlement.

It is desirable that agreement be reached by collective bargaining without mediation assistance. However, public policy and applicable statutes recognize that mediation is the appropriate form of governmen-

189

tal participation in cases where it is required. Whether and when a mediator should intercede will normally be influenced by the desires of the parties. Intercession by a mediator on his own motion should be limited to exceptional cases.

The mediator must not consider himself limited to keeping peace at the bargaining table. His role should be one of being a resource upon which the parties may draw and, when appropriate, he should be prepared to provide both procedural and substantive suggestions and alternatives which will assist the parties in successful negotiations.

Since mediation is essentially a voluntary process, the acceptability of the mediator by the parties as a person of integrity, objectivity, and fairness is absolutely essential to the effective performance of the duties of the mediator. The manner in which the mediator carries out his professional duties and responsibilities will measure his usefulness as a mediator. The quality of his character as well as his intellectual, emotional, social and technical attributes will reveal themselves by the conduct of the mediator and his oral and written communications with the parties, other mediators and the public.

2. The Responsibility of the Mediator Toward Other Mediators

A mediator should not enter any dispute which is being mediated by another mediator or mediators without first conferring with the person or persons conducting such mediation. The mediator should not intercede in a dispute merely because another mediator may also be participating. Conversely, it should not be assumed that the lack of mediation participation by one mediator indicates a need for participation by another mediator.

In those situations where more than one mediator is participating in a particular case, each mediator has a responsibility to keep the others informed of developments essential to a cooperative effort and should extend every possible courtesy to his fellow mediator.

The mediator should carefully avoid any appearance of disagreement with or criticism of his fellow mediator. Discussions as to what positions and actions mediators should take in particular cases should be carried on solely between or among the mediators.

3. The Responsibility of the Mediator Toward His Agency and His Profession

Agencies responsible for providing mediation assistance to parties engaged in collective bargaining are a part of government. The mediator must recognize that, as such, he is part of government. The mediator should constantly bear in mind that he and his work are not judged solely on an individual basis but that he is also judged as a representative of his agency. Any improper conduct or professional shortcoming, therefore, reflects not only on the individual mediator but upon his employer and, as such, jeopardizes the effectiveness of his agency, other government agencies, and the acceptability of the mediation process.

The mediator should not use his position for private gain or advantage, nor should he engage in any employment, activity, or enterprise which will conflict with his work as a mediator, nor should he accept any money or thing of value for the performance of his duties—other than his regular salary—or incur obligations to any party which might interfere with the impartial performance of his duties.

4. The Responsibility of the Mediator Toward the Public

Collective bargaining is in essence a private, voluntary process. The primary purpose of mediation is to assist the parties to achieve a settlement. Such assistance does not abrogate the rights of the parties to resort to economic and legal sanctions. However, the mediation process may include a responsibility to assert the interest of the public that a particular dispute be settled; that a work stoppage be ended; and that normal operations be resumed. It should be understood, however, that the mediator does not regulate or control any of the content of a collective bargaining agreement.

It is conceivable that a mediator might find it necessary to withdraw from a negotiation, if it is patently clear that the parties intend to use his presence as implied governmental sanction for an agreement obviously contrary to public policy.

It is recognized that labor disputes are settled at the bargaining table; however, the mediator may release appropriate information with due regard (1) to the desires of the parties, (2) to whether that information will assist or impede the settlement of the dispute and (3) to the needs of an informed public.

Publicity shall not be used by a mediator to enhance his own position or that of his agency. Where two or more mediators are mediating a dispute, public information should be handled through a mutually agreeable procedure.

5. The Responsibility of the Mediator Toward the Mediation Process

Collective bargaining is an established institution in our economic way of life. The practice of mediation requires the development of alternatives which the parties will voluntarily accept as a basis for settling their problems. Improper pressures which jeopardize voluntary action by the parties should not be a part of mediation.

Since the status, experience, and ability of the mediator lend weight to his suggestions and recommendations, he should evaluate carefully the effect of his suggestions and recommendations and accept full responsibility for their honesty and merit.

The mediator has a continuing responsibility to study industrial relations to improve his skills and upgrade his abilities.

Suggestions by individual mediators or agencies to parties, which give the implication that transfer of a case from one mediation "forum" to another will produce better results, are unprofessional and are to be condemned.

Confidential infomation acquired by the mediator should not be disclosed to others for any purpose or in a legal proceeding or be used directly or indirectly for the personal benefit or profit of the mediator.

Bargaining positions, proposals, or suggestions given to the mediator in confidence during the course of bargaining for his sole information should not be disclosed to the other party without first securing permission from the party or person who gave it to him.

Index